WOMEN AND THE
NOBEL PEACE PRIZE

WOMEN AND THE NOBEL PEACE PRIZE

INGUNN NORDERVAL

Dignity Press
World Dignity University Press

For inquiries about author interviews, in person or via the Internet, by Ingunn Norderval, please contact: inorderval@hotmail.com.

Published by Dignity Press
16 Northview Ct.
Lake Oswego, OR 97035
www.dignitypress.org

Cover design by Kaia Means

Cover images:
All photographs, obtained through
Wikimedia Commons, are in the public domain.

Book website: http://www.dignitypress.org/Nobel-Prize
ISBN: 978-1-952292-04-0
ePub edition: 978-1-952292-05-7
Kindle edition: 978-1-952292-06-4

Contents

Preface by WILPF Norway

Ingrid Eide

During the present decade, several important anniversaries call for celebration. In 2013, it was one hundred years since Norwegian women were given full voting rights on the same basis as men. The following year we celebrated the 200th anniversary of our constitution, one of the oldest in the world. That year was also an occasion for remembering and studying the First World War and its significant consequences. In 2015, Women's International League for Peace and Freedom (WILPF) and its Norwegian section, Internasjonal Kvinneliga for Fred og Frihet (IKFF, now WILPF Norway), could point to one hundred years of continuous work against war and for demilitarization and peace. From the very beginning of its existence, WILPF Norway has emphasized the necessity of building international institutions for nonviolent conflict solutions in order to secure peaceful cooperation among the world's nations and their people.

In the spring of 1915, little more than half a year after the outbreak of the war, over one thousand women from both neutral and warring nations met in the Hague, hoping to put an end to hostilities and create an institutional framework that would prevent future warfare. Both of these endeavours failed: The war continued for another three years and, less than a generation later, the Second World War broke out. Even so, or rather, because of this, peace-loving women have persevered. The Women's International League for Peace and Freedom contributed to the launching of first the League of Nations and then the United Nations. For more than a century, leaders and members of WILPF have continued their work for peace and against war through a vast network of chapters all over the world.

WILPF's program reflected the ideas regarding war and peace that were current at the time of its creation, ideas that the Austrian peace activist and author Bertha von Suttner conveyed to Alfred Nobel, which he included in his will when he decided that part of his fortune should be used to establish a prize in honor of significant work for peace.

In 1905, Bertha von Suttner was the first woman to receive the Nobel Peace Prize. But what about all the other women who spent their energy in all-consuming work for peace? How many were nominated as candidates for the Nobel Peace Prize, and what did their contribution consist of? How were they treated by the Norwegian Nobel Committee? Why did only three women receive the Peace Prize, not only during the first sixty years of the history of the Peace Prize, but, indeed, during the first seventy-five years of its existence? The archives of the Nobel Institute are now open for scrutiny of the first six decades of the twentieth century, which Dr. Norderval's analysis covers. During this period, Jane Addams and Emily Greene Balch, both Americans who had been prominent leaders of WILPF, joined Bertha von Sutter as Peace Prize laureates. During the same years, forty-six men were recipients of the prize.

The Nobel Peace Prize and the nominations received by the Norwegian Nobel Committee reveal prevailing views regarding what promotes peace. WILPF wishes to focus on the contribution women have made in furthering the peace process. The archives at the Nobel Institute represent a valuable source of knowledge about women's work in this area, and WILPF is grateful that Ingunn Norderval conveys the thoughts and experiences of the female Nobel nominees and sheds light on how the Nobel Committee experts explained why the nominees did not deserve a prize for their efforts.

FOREWORD

EVELIN LINDNER & LINDA HARTLING

This is an untold story of the Nobel Peace Prize, often considered the most prestigious prize in the world. While much has been written, very little is generally known about the inner workings of the selection process and even less is known about the women nominated for this award. Although women comprise over half of the world's population, few people know of the contributions women have made to advance peace around the globe. Even fewer know that it was a woman who encouraged the establishment of the Nobel Peace Prize. Celebrated Austrian peace activist and author Bertha von Suttner corresponded with Alfred Nobel until the last days of his life, and many believe that this played the major role in influencing his decision to include the Peace Prize in his will.

From the perspective of our research, this book enlightens readers about one of the most insidious forms of humiliation: *being treated as invisible.* Invisibility is a common condition experienced by oppressed and marginalized groups, and it is a stubbornly pervasive experience for women. Throughout history, women's full participation in society has been limited by the prevailing view that women's work is for the most part unworthy of notice. Women's efforts have gone unsupported, restricted to domestic spheres, undervalued, demeaned, and discounted, even when women have been at the center of the most important work in the world, raising the next generation. This is the tragedy of invisibility.

Peace workers, too, are casualties of invisibility. Their efforts rarely garner grandiose attention, textbook documentation, or accolades. There are few monuments to peace, few memorials to veteran peace workers, few buildings named for peace activists, and few statues of peace heroes (please check your own community). Peace workers are rarely rewarded or supported for their efforts, and we suspect this has to do with peace not necessarily being a pathway to profit for a number of powerful entities. Indeed, today's "military industrial complex" gorges itself on endless wars, generating what we might call nuclear bombs of profit. Despite this, peace workers persist.

Women peace workers must navigate some of the deepest waters of humiliation. They aren't valued for their peace work *and* they aren't valued as women. This book reveals that the groundbreaking efforts of women Nobel Peace Prize nominees were underestimated, overlooked, discounted, treated with suspicion, demeaned, and rejected. Eleanor Roosevelt, in particular, comes to mind. Her credentials included chairing the committee that drafted one of the most important proclamations of the last century, namely, the United Nations Universal Declaration of Human Rights in 1948. Although she was nominated for the Prize four times, she was not deemed worthy, even in 1948 when no one was presented with the award. Her story is one among many in this book that need to be remembered.

Dr. Lindner met Ingunn Norderval in 2016 at a gathering organized by one of her mentors, the late Trine Eklund. Trine was a leader in the Norwegian peace movement, including the "Nordic Women's Peace Marches" against nuclear weapons in Europe in 1981, in the USSR in 1982, and the USA in 1983. She also headed the Norwegian Peace Council, an umbrella organization for about 20 peace organizations. Trine introduced me to the Norwegian edition of Norderval's book, *Nobelkomiteen og kvinnene* (The Nobel Committee and the Women), published in 2015 by the Norwegian branch of the Women's International League for Peace and Freedom (WILPF), on the occasion of its 100th anniversary. This was the start of our efforts to develop an English translation of this remarkable book.

Together with the help of Linda Hartling and Jane Hilken, this book became a proud project of Dignity Press, the publishing branch of Human Dignity and Humiliation Studies (HumanDHS) that is also home to the World Dignity University initiative. HumanDHS is a global transdisciplinary network and collaborative community of concerned scholars, researchers, educators, practitioners, artists, and others who wish to stimulate systemic change, globally and locally, to open space for peace and mutual dignity to take root and grow. Our goal is ending humiliating practices, preventing new ones from arising, and creating space for feelings of humiliation to be transformed into action that saves lives and may save the world.

Reading about the courageous efforts of the women described in the book gives us the courage to keep moving forward with our work. We hope it will inspire all who work for peace and dignity in the world!

INTRODUCTION BY THE AUTHOR

INGUNN NORDERVAL

When Bertha von Suttner published *Die Waffen Nieder* (Lay Down Your Arms) in 1889, the book became an immense success and helped contribute to the rise of a strong peace movement in the western world at the turn of the century. The many wars during the 1800s, the Napoleonic wars, the Crimean war, the bloody American Civil War, and the French-Prussian war, had created revulsion against the barbarism that war represents and a deeply felt desire for peaceful resolution of conflicts among states.

The Swedish inventor and businessman Alfred Nobel became one of von Suttner's admirers, and in his will he stipulated that part of his fortune should finance a prize to be given to "the person who shall have done the most or the best work for fraternity between nations, for the abolition or reduction of standing armies and for the holding and promotion of peace congresses."[1] This "peace prize" would be awarded by a committee appointed by the Norwegian parliament. Four other prizes, in literature, medicine, physics, and chemistry, would be awarded by Swedish institutions.

Many people in the peace movement had expected Bertha von Suttner to be the first recipient of the Nobel Peace Prize. However, the Norwegian Nobel Committee chose to overlook her for several years, in spite of the fact that she was nominated every year from 1901 to 1905 and that her candidature had enormous support.

In the years that followed, few women appeared worthy to become Nobel laureates. Over the course of seventy-five years, only three were awarded the prize. Since women played such a prominent role in the organized peace movement throughout the twentieth century, it seems legitimate to ask: Why were so few women honored by the Nobel Committee? Were women the victims of discrimination? Who were those very few women who were nominated as Nobel Peace Prize candidates?

It is questions such as these I pose in my book, which covers the first six decades of the history of the Nobel Peace Prize. In addition to Bertha von Suttner, Jane Addams, and Emily Greene Balch, the three Prize laureates, all the other thirty-three women who were nominated for the prize during this period will be presented.

Many of these women were prominent personalities, who deserve to be remembered. Still, most of them are forgotten. My purpose is to relate their stories and the work they accomplished to help build a less violent world. Unfortunately, very little source material exists for some of the women peace pioneers. In the case of a few of them, the Nobel Institute's archive includes only some short, handwritten letters. Consequently, this results in an imbalance in the biographical notes, with relatively broad presentations of some of the candidates, but, unfortunately, very brief commentaries regarding others. For a few of the women it has even been impossible to obtain such vital data as the dates of their births and deaths.

The Norwegian Nobel Committee's work has been analyzed by many writers over the years, but none appear to have been especially interested in exploring the almost total absence of women among the laureates until the most recent period. It is my intention to shed some light on the "forgotten candidates," the thirty-three female nominees who did not become Nobel laureates during the years from 1901 to 1960. The Appendices include short comments on the fourteen women who have won the Peace Prize between 1960 and 2020.

Special thanks go to the staff at the library at the Norwegian Nobel Institute, and in particular to Anne C. Kjelling, for their help in locating literature that has made possible the content in this book. A travel grant from The Norwegian Non-Fiction Writers and Translators enabled me to work for some time at the New York Public Library. Thanks also go to WILPF Norway for its publication of the book, and especially to Mari Holmboe Ruge and Ingrid Eide for their support and encouragement. Their many useful commentaries were invaluable. I also want to express thanks to François Gacougnolle and my daughter, Kaia Means, for their help in getting the manuscript finished.

This revised edition is translated by me from Norwegian to English. I am deeply grateful to Evelin Lindner, Linda Hartling, and Jane Hilken for their active engagement in the process of editing the manuscript and getting it ready for publication. Finally, thanks to Dr. Han van Bree of the Netherlands, for his generosity in sharing valuable information regarding Barbara Waylen's participation in the European peace movement after World War Two.

Chapter 1
The Background for the Nobel Peace Prize

It created considerable concern when Alfred Nobel's will became known after his death in Italy on December 10, 1896. As already mentioned, Nobel had decided that his enormous fortune should constitute the basis of a fund that would award annual international prizes in five fields: literature, medicine, chemistry, physics, and work toward peace. The first four of these prizes would be awarded by Swedish institutions, while the last would be awarded by a committee appointed by the Norwegian parliament.

Nobel's relatives were furious and received whole-hearted support from King Oscar II, who publicly criticized Nobel and encouraged the family to get the will declared invalid. The Peace Prize was a particular source of irritation to the king, who wrote to Nobel's nephew, Emanuel Nobel, that his uncle had come under the influence of irresponsible idealists and, especially, women.[1] Fortunately, neither the king nor others succeeded in their attempts to set the will of Alfred Nobel aside. Scientists, writers, and peace workers from all continents have been beneficiaries of Nobel's generous gift, and the Nobel Peace Prize is described as the world's most prestigious prize in *Oxford Dictionary of Contemporary History*.[2] The first woman to become a Peace Prize laureate was Bertha von Suttner in

1905. Well over a quarter century later, in 1931, another woman, the famous American social worker Jane Addams, shared the prize with her fellow countryman Nicholas Murray Butler. In 1946, another American, Dr. Emily Greene Balch, shared the prize with John Mott. Then, a whole generation was to pass before the "Irish Peace Women," Mairead Corrigan and Betty Williams, brought the number of female laureates up to five, in 1976. Since then, twelve more women have been honored.

A total of 128 Nobel Peace Prizes were awarded between 1901 and 2014, sixteen to women, eighty-seven to men and twenty-five to organizations (see tables in the Appendix). The Red Cross has received the prize three times, in 1917, 1944, and 1963. Among other international organizations that have been Prize recipients are The Institute of International Law, The International Peace Bureau, The International Labour Organization (ILO), and UNICEF.

The world's oldest continuously existing women's peace organization, the Women's International League for Peace and Freedom (WILPF) has been nominated for the Prize several times. In spite of the fact that WILPF, perhaps more than any other organization, has aimed tirelessly to attain just those goals Nobel mentioned as criteria for awarding the Peace Prize, namely, fraternity among nations, armament reduction, and arrangement of peace conferences, the organization has never been honored by the Nobel Committee. Many of the women nominated for the Prize during the period 1901–1960 were founding members of WILPF and held leading positions in the organization. Alva Myrdal, who received the Nobel Peace Prize in 1982, was also an active WILPF member.

Beginning the year after Nobel's death, there were several candidates for the Prize. Some suggested their own candidacy. Carl Kongerød from Skien in Norway, for instance, announced he was an applicant for at least three of the Nobel prizes. H. Grimm from Russia wrote that he applied for the Peace Prize in order to build a "mission house for world peace." A Norwegian immigrant to the United States, Nils O. Rørsen, announced cheerfully that he "demanded the Nobel prize" because of his unpublished essay, "The Protection of World Peace." He attached his Norwegian baptismal certificate to the "application." Another Norwegian applied for support since he had been injured in a dynamite explosion.

We also find a woman's name among these early letters. Henriette Verdier Winteler de Weindeck announced her interest in the "various criteria concerning the peace prize" in 1897. She was later nominated in 1905 by a member of the French parliament, Gerville Reache, on the grounds that she "wrote about peace." In 1907 and 1910, parliamentarians from Portugal nominated de Weindeck because she had written a book about peace and disarmament.

Before the first Nobel Peace Prize award in 1901, clear guidelines were adopted as to who was entitled to nominate candidates for the prize and what criteria were relevant for the candidatures. This put an end to "beggars" and more or less curious nominations. The Committee also agreed on effective routines for dealing with the proposals submitted, such as establishing a so-called "shortlist" of the most interesting candidates among the nominees, whose merits would then be subjected to closer scrutiny by the committee members.

THE SHORTLIST

When the Nobel Committee meets to decide who is to be the year's Nobel Prize laureate, its consultants have prepared biographical essays on all of the candidates picked out for the shortlist. No records are kept of the Committee's deliberations, and the biographies submitted to the Nobel Committee by the consultants are available to the public only after fifty years have passed. This material constitutes a large part of the sources I have relied on in order to sketch the profiles of the thirty-six women who were candidates for the Nobel Peace Prize during the first six decades of the twentieth century. For a few of the women, this is the only information I have been able to find. For others, a considerable amount of writing exists. Hence, there is a lack of balance in the presentations, with some of the candidates receiving more attention than others. Of course, this also reflects the varied background and influence of the candidates. Eleanor Roosevelt, Alexandra Kollontay, Rosika Schwimmer and Carrie Chapman Catt, to mention just a few, are examples of towering personalities who may have been passed over by the Norwegian Nobel Committee simply because they were women.

During the first decade of the 1900s, only two women, Bertha von Suttner from Austria and Great Britain's Priscilla Hannah Peckover, earned a place on the shortlist. During the same period, a total of forty men were awarded this honor. In 1913, Priscilla Peckover was again to be found on the shortlist, together with the American peace activist Lucia Ames Mead. The following year, in 1914, the prominent American lawyer Belva Ann Lockwood was on the shortlist together with eleven men. The next woman to make it to the shortlist was also an American: The internationally famous social reformer Jane Addams was nominated and put on the shortlist in 1916. She was to be nominated another seven times before finally being honored with the Nobel Peace Prize in 1931. By that time she was in failing health and could not make the trip to Oslo to accept the Prize.

As already mentioned, only thirty-six women were found among the over one thousand nominees for the Peace Prize during the period from 1901 to 1960. Just three of these thirty-six became Nobel laureates. After the Second World War, more women were nominated, and several were also placed on the shortlist for evaluation, among them Eleanor Roosevelt and the Soviet Union's Alexandra Kollontay.

But it wasn't until 1976 that the coveted Prize would go once more to women. What common features did these thirty-six women share? More than anything, it is their radicalism that comes to mind. For many of them the path to peace activism started with a deep commitment to the cause of women's rights through voting rights associations and women's political parties. They were outspoken feminists and radical social critics. Most of the American women Nobel nominees during this first half of the twentieth century were outspoken critics of capitalism and declared their belief in social democracy.

For some, their antiwar views led to an uncompromising pacifism, and many were active members of the Women's League for Peace and Freedom (WILPF), the organization that through its information activity and arranging of peace conferences aspired to realize Alfred Nobel's ideals probably more than any other group.

SOME CENTRAL QUESTIONS

Since peace work traditionally has engaged more women than men, it appears curious that so few women have received the Nobel Peace Prize. Were, perhaps, the wording and terms of Nobel's will such that women were excluded per definition as candidates? Were women proposed to a lesser degree than men? Or were they simply overlooked by the Committee itself? After all, until 1949 the Norwegian Nobel Committee consisted exclusively of men, and there were no women among the directors or consultants at the Nobel Institute.

However, first and foremost: Who were the few women who became peace laureates or were nominated as candidates for the Peace Prize? What was their background? What was the nature of their work for peace?

Answers to some of these questions may perhaps be found

in the reasons given by the people who nominated the candidates for the Prize and in the recommendations of the consultants charged with preparing the materials for the members of the Nobel Committee prior to their decision. The archives at the Nobel Institute in Oslo constitute the most important sources of information for this book.

The first hypothesis, that the wording of Nobel's will could have the effect of excluding women simply because of their gender, may be dismissed immediately. Alfred Nobel wrote simply that the fifth prize should go to the person who had done the most to influence fraternity among the world's peoples, to diminish military might, and to work for peace by arranging peace congresses. There is nothing here which in and of itself excludes women.

There have been claims that Nobel assumed that his friend, the author and peace activist Bertha von Suttner, would be the first recipient of the prize. It therefore appears appropriate to direct attention to the nominations that were made during the period examined and the evaluations that the consultants produced for the Nobel Committee prior to its decisions.

As already mentioned, during the first sixty years of the history of the Nobel Peace Prize, only three women were to be found among the laureates. Was this due to outright discrimination? Statistics seem to acquit the Nobel Committee of this suspicion. Very few women were nominated during the period 1901–1960. Of the thirty-six women nominated, some of them several times, sixteen, or well over 40 percent, were placed on the committee's shortlist. This was a far higher proportion than the men could boast of. Further: almost one-fifth of the women who were evaluated, three out of sixteen, received the Peace Prize. This number is also relatively higher than the corresponding number for men. Both in 1931 and 1946, all the female nominees slipped through the needle's eye and earned a spot on the Committee's shortlists. In 1931, this included

Jane Addams, Lady Aberdeen, and Annie Besant and, in 1946, Emily Greene Balch and Alexandra Kollontay.

The low number of female prize winners must therefore be ascribed first of all to women's general position in society during this period. Prior to World War One, only four countries in the whole world had granted women the right to vote on the same terms as men in national elections, namely Australia, New Zealand, Finland, and Norway. As late as at the outbreak of World War Two, a great many nations still denied women the right to vote. Naturally, this was reflected in the power women had to exercise influence in their societies. They had, to put it shortly, very little opportunity to meet the criteria stipulated as conditions for the right to propose candidates for the Nobel Peace Prize. This was the prerogative of parliamentarians, cabinet ministers, professors of social science, history, law, and theology, members of international courts and national supreme courts, earlier Nobel Prize laureates, and the Nobel Peace Prize Committee itself. Relatively few women were to be found within the circles of these august elites.

Even so, many of the women nominees during these early days were prominent people in their various fields of competence and performed such an outstanding contribution to the cause of peace that it seems rather curious that they were not found worthy of the Peace Prize. Professor Irwin Abrams, internationally known for his works on the Nobel Prize winners, acknowledges[3] that it probably was "the spirit of the time" that was most to blame for the fact that so few women were awarded the Prize. However, he also notes that one should have been able to expect more from the Committee:

> The inadequacies in the earlier record are more a reflection upon our civilization in general than upon the Norwegian Nobel Committee in particular, but since it was a woman who had so much to do with Nobel's

setting up the award in the first place, one might some-how have expected better of the committee.[4]

In a later article he suggests that "…it would seem that the Committees were not without prejudice."[5] Professor Burton Feldman supports this view in an analysis of the work of the Nobel Committee during the first decades of the twentieth century: "Pacifism and feminism were often early com-rades-in-arms, and deserved more recognition by the Nobel Committee."[6]

Many of the women Peace Prize candidates were without doubt very committed feminists who over the years had worked hard for universal voting rights, the improvement of women's situation in the occupational world, and for their equal access to education at all levels as well as the right to social and po-litical positions. Closely tied to their feminist convictions was their engagement in areas that historically had been looked at as women's tasks, care for children and youngsters and for those occupying the lowest ladders of society. Many of the women identified themselves as radicals and demanded a fundamental change in society's economic structures, which in their opinion created inequality and a basis for conflict both nationally and internationally. Thus, peace work became a logical extension of their feminism, their social responsibility, and radical atti-tudes. However, feminism and radicalism were not qualities that worked to their advantage when they were to be evaluated as candidates for the Nobel Peace Prize.

One senses a certain amount of condescension reflected in many of the commentaries by the consultants who prepared the agenda for the Nobel Committee and wrote the short bi-ographies of the candidates that Committee members were to consider. An example of this is clearly evident in the case of Lady Aberdeen, longtime leader of the World Council of Women. The consultant points out that her candidature was primarily supported by female peace activists. In the case of others, fear was expressed regarding their radicalism. Possible negative reactions in Great Britain were, for example, noted in connection with the nomination of Annie Besant in 1931. Her active support for the nationalist independence movement in India was perceived as regular treason by many Britons.

Even though it would be incorrect to accuse the Nobel Committee of outright discrimination of women, there is ample ground to suspect that the women who were candidates during the course of the first sixty years of its history were in some cases unfairly evaluated, and consequently passed over.

Chapter 2
The Period 1901–1940

Bertha von Suttner (1843–1914)

The story of Bertha von Suttner and her friendship with and influence on Alfred Nobel is so well known that it will not be retold here. Let us just recapitulate a few facts: Bertha von Suttner belonged to the Austrian nobility and held the title of Baroness von Kinsky before her marriage to Arthur von Suttner in 1876. She had been hired as governess to the daughters of the family and fell head-over-heels in love with the son of the house. However, since she was poor and belonged to the lesser nobility, she was not considered to be a desirable daughter-in-law. Bertha went to Paris where she worked for Alfred Nobel for about a week in 1876 after having responded to his advertisement seeking a secretary. A telegram from Arthur von Suttner made her return to Austria. The couple got married secretly and left immediately for the Caucasus, where they lived for nearly a decade. It was here that Bertha von Suttner began her career as a writer. In 1888, she published her first book, *Das Machinenzeitalter* (The Machine Age). The book was published under a pseudonym, since her husband was afraid that it would not be read if a woman's name was displayed on the title page. Only when the book was issued the third time, in 1899, did von

Suttner's own name appear on the title page. By that time, Bertha von Suttner had already attained world fame for another book, *Die Waffen Nieder!* (Lay Down Your Arms!). This book was published in 1889, was reprinted several times, and was translated into many languages.

After Bertha and Arthur von Suttner returned to Austria in 1885, Bertha got increasingly involved in peace work. She was one of the founders of the Austrian Peace Union and served as its leader for many years. She also became a central figure in the international peace movement, and through her friendship with Alfred Nobel, she obtained generous donations for the cause of peace. The Norwegian historians Stenersen, Libæk, and Sveen declare: "There is little doubt that the baroness has much of the credit for Alfred Nobel's decision to establish a peace prize."[1] Bertha von Suttner was nominated as a Peace Prize candidate every year from 1901 to 1905, when she finally obtained the Prize. Women's associations, both in Scandinavia and other countries, professors, and prominent peace activists supported her candidacy; in 1904, she received many more proposals than any other candidate. The Committee still chose to overlook her and awarded the Prize to the Institute of International Law, something that caused widespread criticism. Among the strongest critics was the popular Norwegian author Bjørnstjerne Bjørnson.

The longtime secretary of the Norwegian Nobel Committee, Ragnvald Moe, suggested in an interview in 1960 that a possible reason for overlooking von Suttner for several years was the fear that giving her the Prize would be perceived as an important symbolic victory for the Norwegian feminist movement, which at the time was very controversial.[2] Halvdan Koht, who later became Norway's foreign secretary, was the Committee consultant both in 1904 and 1905. In his report to the Committee in 1904, he admitted that Bertha von Suttner had received a great deal of support, but added that hardly any of the proposals included adequate explanations as to why she deserved the Prize and that many were totally irrelevant, focusing mostly on her age, health, and financial situation. The following year, his summary to the Committee includes a reference to the Austrian nobleman von Pirquet, who was rumored to stand behind a coordinated support for von Suttner. Koht also alleged that many of the nominations had identical wording.

Koht is very likely correct in regard to some of his observations. They nevertheless seem petty, since Bertha von Suttner was neither the first nor the last nominee for candidates of the Peace Prize to experience organized campaign activity on her behalf. Stenersen, Libæk, and Sveen suggest that unconscious discriminatory attitudes may have contributed to the delay in giving her the Prize:

> The Committee may have thought that she unduly drew attention to her own influence on Alfred Nobel, thus suspecting her of promoting her own candidature. She was also a woman in a strongly male-dominated movement. Furthermore, several of the pre-1905 winners were aging men; the Committee wished to honor them before it was too late.[3]

Bertha von Suttner came to Kristiania (today's Oslo) in the spring of 1906 to deliver her Nobel lecture. Women's organizations constituted an important part of the celebration, and a women's choir and orchestra performed in her honor. She was received in audience both by King Haakon of Norway and his brother, King Christian of Denmark. Eight years later, on the eve of the outbreak of World War I, Bertha von Suttner died before the stark forces erupted that she had spent a lifetime fighting against.

JANE ADDAMS (1860–1935)

The second woman to receive the Nobel Peace Prize, Jane Addams, was also passed by several times. Her name was placed before the Committee for the first time in 1916. When she finally received the Prize in 1931, it was the eighth time she was nominated. Irwin Abrams does not mince words when he comments on this: "The Oslo committees need not have waited so long to honour Jane Addams."[4] The Norwegian historian Asle Sveen agrees:

> One would think that Jane Addams would have been the ideal Peace Prize winner in 1916, but the committee decided against awarding a prize that year. One may ask why, but it is likely that women's issues were not high on its list of priorities. In 1917, long-standing Nobel Committee adviser Halvdan Koht wrote a summary of the peace initiatives made until then, with no mention of either Jane Addams or The Hague women's conference of 1915. Koht knew Addams. He met and spoke with her when he visited Hull House before the war.[5]

Irwin Abrams is also of the opinion that it would have been right to give the prize to Addams in 1916: "The most appropriate moment for the award would have been in 1916, when she was leading a spectacular movement to promote mediation between the belligerents of the First World War."[6] In 1923, Jane Addams had massive support among those entitled to nominate candidates—again, the Nobel Committee abstained from appointing a winner. Abrams uses blunt language when he criticizes the Committee for not honoring Addams until she was nearing the end of her life and then giving her only "half the prize."[7] She had to share the prize with Nicholas Murray Butler, the president of Columbia University.

It is interesting to read the evaluations Addams received by the consultants to the Nobel Committee. Although positive, they reflected condescending attitudes to women political activists, as this comment in 1916: "Miss Addams does not go to extremes in her reform policies. She avoids the reefs on which so many female politicians run aground, namely, the demand to see their ideal realized immediately."[8] The consultant commends Addams for her moderation, but also repeats charges that she only joins a cause when victory is already in sight, without mentioning the unfairness of such attacks, considering Addams' long service in the movement for social reform, the women's movement, and the peace movement.

Jane Addams grew up in a wealthy Illinois family and received a good education. After finishing college, she founded the famous center named Hull House in Chicago, where poverty-stricken immigrants got help as they tried to find their way in a new and unfamiliar society. When the Spanish-American war broke out in 1898, Addams, like so many other women, found their way from involvement with social reform to active engagement in the peace movement, and in 1907, she published her book *Newer Ideals of Peace*. By now, Addams had won national acclaim for her work. She received an honorary doctoral degree from the University of Wisconsin in 1904, and in 1910, she became the first woman ever to be awarded an honorary doctoral degree at Yale. When Theodore Roosevelt ran for office as the presidential candidate of the Progressive Party in 1912, Addams delivered the nominating speech at the party congress. She also campaigned actively for his election, even though she herself could not vote. Not until the 1920 passage of the 19th Amendment to the Constitution, did American women get voting rights on the same basis as men.

The outbreak of the world war made Addams, together with other feminist friends, start a new party in the United States. The Woman's Peace Party was launched in 1915 with

Addams as its leader. The same year, she was elected president of the Women's Peace Congress that met at The Hague during the last three days of April. Over one thousand women, representing twelve nations, assembled in protest against the war. The Peace Congress adopted important resolutions regarding the need for permanent international mediation institutions and strongly advocated the creation of a league of nations to be established as a bulwark against future wars. In order to secure continuity in peace work, the Peace Congress decided to establish The International Committee of Women for Permanent Peace (ICWPP) with Jane Addams as leader. Also, the Woman's Peace Party became an American section within ICWPP, and the most important parts of its program were adopted as the basis for the work of the new peace organization.

After her return to the United States, Jane Addams visited President Wilson at the White House several times in an attempt to persuade him to assume the mantle of leadership and assemble a world conference of political leaders against the war. She did not succeed.

It was an enormous disappointment for Addams when the United States entered the war in 1917. As an uncompromising pacifist, she was very critical of the American war effort, something which affected her standing among her fellow citizens. She was, says Asle Sveen, "transformed from peace saint to national threat."[9] When she finally got the Nobel Peace Prize in 1931, she was too old and ill to make a transatlantic trip. She died four years later in 1935.

OTHER CANDIDATES (1901–1940)

As already pointed out, very few women were nominated for the Nobel Peace Prize during these early years. Even fewer were awarded a place on the Nobel Committee's shortlist. From 1900 to 1920, only five women earned such status. In addition to Bertha von Suttner and Jane Addams, Britain's Priscilla Hannah Peckover and the two prominent American peace activists, Lucia Ames Mead and Belva Ann Lockwood, were placed on the shortlist. During the same two decades, six more women were candidates for the Prize.

PRISCILLA HANNAH PECKOVER (1833–1931)

Priscilla Hannah Peckover was born in the little town of Wisbech in Norfolk, England, where she lived all her life. The family belonged to the Quakers, and Priscilla remained a lifelong member of the Quaker Society. As a young girl, she became an ardent teetotaller as well as an active opponent of the slave trade and a supporter of the abolitionist movement. However, starting in the 1870s, the peace movement absorbed her totally, requiring all of her time. In 1879, she started a local peace society in Wisbech, whose membership shortly grew to include more than 6,500 people. She also published her own paper, *Peace and Goodwill*, which was entirely financed by her. Already in 1905, she was nominated for the Peace Prize.

Christian L. Lange, who was then a young consultant to the Nobel Committee, wrote the report on Peckover and described the peace activities in Wisbech as completely due to her work. He also pointed to the fact that she alone was responsible for the funding of the peace society and underscored her total selflessness. She preferred to work quietly behind the curtains; "one very seldom finds her name in *Peace and Goodwill*, even though it is published by her," writes Lange.[10]

A strong religious faith constituted the basis for Peckover's peace activism and her absolute pacifism, which made her also condemn defensive war. Compared to the far more internationally acclaimed Bertha von Suttner, Peckover's contribution to the peace movement was of lesser dimensions, but through her generous financial support of peace groups outside of England, especially in the Nordic countries, she undoubtedly played a valuable role in the growth of peace organizations. She also understood the Scandinavian languages and translated Nordic peace literature into English.

Priscilla Hannah Peckover was proposed as a Nobel Prize laureate twice more, in 1911 and 1913; in 1913, she was again placed on the shortlist, this time in the company of Lucia Ames Mead from Massachusetts, USA. Neither of them obtained the prestigious Prize.

LUCIA AMES MEAD (1856–1936)

One of the most prominent American peace activists during the first decades of the twentieth century was Lucia Ames Mead. She was born in Boscawen, New Hampshire, spent her childhood in Chicago, and moved to Boston at the age of 14. There, she studied theology and philosophy, literature and politics, and became a member of the city's intellectual elite. The American poet Ralph Waldo Emerson exercised great influence on her development, as did Jane Addams, whose views on the need for social reform she shared. In the circle around Emerson, she also met her future husband, Edwin Mead, whom she married in 1898. Edwin Mead was one of New England's most prominent intellectual leaders. As a philosopher, author, and antimilitarist, he was a well-known spokesman for the peace movement and for conflict resolution in international affairs.

The marriage between Lucia and Edwin Mead was a partnership based on mutual respect and equality and a passion for social reform and peace work. The couple published various peace journals, and together with a friend, they founded a peace academy in Boston, the International School of Peace. Two years later, the World Peace Foundation was launched, with Edwin Mead as a very active president. The couple travelled extensively all over America as well as in Europe to advance the cause of peace. In 1913, they were jointly nominated for the Peace Prize and placed on the shortlist.

The report to the Nobel Committee written by its consultant, Mikael Lie, does not give a very clear picture of Lucia Ames Mead. Several pages are devoted to Edwin Mead's contribution to the cause of peace, while only one page is spent on Lucia, who consistently "in writing and speech has helped Mead in his peace work."[11] It is evident that he relegates Lucia Ames Mead to the role of the supportive little wife of a much superior husband. This is in stark contrast to the presentation of Lucia Ames Mead by her biographer, John M. Craig.

According to Craig, Ames Mead was "the most well-known peace activist in the United States" during the early part of the twentieth century,[12] and he states unequivocally that "…it would be wrong to assume that Lucia Mead achieved her notable career as a peace advocate simply because she married a person who himself became a leading light of the peace movement."[13] What Lucia accomplished, he assures the readers, she did "primarily on her own because of her own hard work and talent."[14] He also points to Jane Addams' opinion that nobody measured up to Lucia Mead with regard to peace work in America during the years before World War I.[15]

As a volunteer in the slum areas of Boston, Lucia Ames Mead became convinced early of the need for social reforms. In numerous articles she argued that lawlessness and crime were rooted in poverty and lack of opportunity and that reforms in the areas of education, housing policy, and social welfare were needed. In 1898, she published her book *To Whom Much is Given,* where she expressed her increasing scepticism against capitalism and argued for a gradual development toward a social democratic society. Environmental problems, deforestation of vast areas, and river pollution as well as recurring epidemics because of poor social conditions all contributed to her radicalization and views quite consistent with those advocated by Christian Socialists in Europe and the English Fabian Society. Six demands were central to her:

1. Public control, but not necessarily ownership, of important means of production and distribution, such as for instance, mines and the railroads.
2. Abolition of unemployment.
3. An eight-hour work day.
4. Tax policies that prevent accumulation of enormous fortunes.
5. Progressive income tax.
6. Good schooling for all children, and prohibition of child labor.

The same year that Lucia published her book, 1898, the Russian tsar, Nicholas II, issued his proposal for an international demilitarization conference to be held in The Hague. Lucia was captivated by the idea, and in both her speech and writing, she encouraged Americans to support the endeavour. She got only lukewarm response, but she herself was present at both the first Hague conference in 1899 and the second in 1907. In September 1901, she had attended the tenth Universal Peace Congress in Glasgow, Scotland, where she played a very active role in the debates and in the framing of the resolutions passed. She also expressed harsh criticism of President McKinley's role in the Spanish American war, calling it a shameful example of an imperialist policy whose only purpose was to serve American sugar and tobacco interests and their oppression of the native population.

After the Glasgow conference, Lucia Ames Mead became a "professional pacifist" who was on regular speaking tours in both Europe and the United States up to the outbreak of war in 1914. In 1903, she was elected president of the Massachusetts Woman Suffrage Association, and in her speeches and newspaper articles, she especially tried to influence women to become active in peace work, seeing a clear connection between women's possibilities for political participation and the realization of a powerful peace movement.

Besides including women, she insisted that the peace organizations had to cast their net far wider and build alliances with labor unions, church societies, socialist groups, and others who were likely to have positive attitudes toward the peace movement. She felt, however, that the peace organizations in the United States were extremely elitist in their attitudes and were not interested in her efforts to recruit new adherents through appeals to the masses at the grass roots.

Consistent with her belief that it was necessary to reach "the common folk who are our strongest asset,"[16] Mead was also a pioneer in the effort to recruit children as participants in the peace movement. She approached a young female composer and asked her to write a feisty march for kids, a march that would make them understand that firemen, police, and health workers were the real heroes of the country. This, she said, would be a sound and much needed counter-force to all the military marches youngsters were exposed to.

One of Mead's most interesting proposals, also met with thundering silence, was that the federal government should establish a peace budget: "If the United States, which spent millions of dollars on military defence, would set aside the cost of one large battleship to help foster international understanding and aid the work of peace advocates, the need for military expenditures would decrease," she predicted.[17]

After the end of World War I, when women from the entire world met in Zürich in an attempt to exercise some influence on the peace agreements, Lucia Ames Mead was an active participant at the conference. It was here that the Women's International League for Peace and Freedom (WILPF) was formally founded, as the International Committee of Women for Permanent Peace (ICWPP) changed its name. The Woman's Peace Party became the American Section of WILPF, with Lucia Mead as its national secretary. For years she labored intensely to secure ratification by the United States of the League of Nations, writing weekly articles for around one hundred daily newspapers in support of the League. Her articles also appeared in magazines such as the *New Republic, Woman's Journal,* and *New England Magazine.* John Craig estimates that over 90 percent of her writings had to do with the cause of international peace.

Lucia Ames Mead died in 1936, very disillusioned with the American Congress and its politicians. She condemned both the big political parties as morally bankrupt.

BELVA ANN LOCKWOOD (1830–1917)

The very first year that the Nobel Peace Prize was awarded, an American woman was among the nominees. Belva Ann Lockwood was nominated by several members of the U.S. Senate both in 1901 and 1902, but did not attract much attention from the Nobel Peace Committee. In 1914, however, she was on the Committee's shortlist, the second American woman to do so, and only the fourth woman to be so honored in the history of the prize.

Belva Ann Lockwood was a lawyer, practiced law in Washington, D.C., and was married to the Baptist minister Ezekiel Lockwood. Her choice of profession, and the fact that a minister's wife pursued her own career, reveals a determined and liberated woman. The Nobel Committee consultant in 1914 acknowledges that she had "participated very much in the women's movement in the United States."[18] However, his short presentation of the nominee gives no inkling of what a formidable person she really was.

Belva Ann Lockwood was the daughter of a farmer, and

when she was only 14 years old she began teaching at a small rural school. Her father could not, or would not, help her get any further education, and at the age of 18, she got married. Four years later she was widowed and responsible for bringing up a small daughter. She resumed her teaching career, at the same time as she completed a college degree with excellent results.

After moving to Washington, D.C., Belva married Ezekiel Lockwood, several years her senior, and began law studies at one of the few universities that let women enter their premises. She finished her studies in 1872 when she was 42, but her fellow male students were so incensed at the thought of a woman practicing law that they prevailed upon the university administration to deny her a degree certificate. Belva resolutely took her case to President Ulysses S. Grant, who was president of the university's board of governors. With her degree in hand, she opened her own law office in Washington in 1873.[19] A couple of years later she sought permission to argue cases before the Supreme Court, only to encounter opposition once more: The court denied her request on the ground that such a step required congressional legislation.

So, Belva became a lobbyist. She approached members of Congress and managed to persuade enough of them to secure passage of "an act to relieve the legal disabilities of women" in 1879. The next year Belva Ann Lockwood was the first woman to argue a case before the Supreme Court of the United States.

American women did not, of course, possess the right to vote at this time. But Belva Lockwood decided to confront the male establishment and "threw her hat in the ring" as a presidential candidate both in 1884 and 1888 for the National Equal Rights Party. "I cannot vote, but I can be voted for," was her brazen slogan.[20]

Belva Ann Lockwood was by now already well known for her active participation over many years in both the national and international peace movement. When the Universal Peace Union was launched in 1866 by disciples of William Lloyd Garrison and his doctrine of nonviolence, she signed up as a member. She was one of the organization's most respected spokespersons, its leading essayist and lobbyist, and eventually she became its vice president. In 1899 she participated in the World Congress of Peace in Paris and led the deliberations of the American delegation. Back home in the United States, she founded a section of the International Peace Bureau in America and ran its office, for the most part with her own money.

The report on this woman in the archives of the Nobel Committee gives no hint of her stature during her many years of active work for peace. The consultant in 1914 admits that she had made a valuable contribution as a member of the American peace movement, but ends his comments in the following, rather condescending fashion: "She has participated in several world peace conferences, but without playing any role in their deliberations. As for her numerous brochures, I find no reason to say anything about them."[21]

The Norwegian Nobel Committee did not award any prize in 1914. It ought to have given more serious attention to the accomplishments of the first America woman to be nominated for the Peace Prize. Frøydis Eleonora Veseth speculates that a possible reason why the Committee acted the way it did, was its fear of provoking the United States, where Lockwood was a controversial figure: "Lockwood was likely too radical to be considered as a possible recipient of the peace prize. The main problem for her was probably that she acted like a man while everyone else expected her to act like a woman."[22]

HENRIETTE VERDIER WINTELER DE WEINDECK

In addition to the women who were placed on the Nobel Committee's shortlist during these first decades, several others were nominated as candidates. The first of them, Henriette Verdier Winteler de Weindeck from Portugal, had herself written to the Committee already in 1897 with inquiries regarding the different criteria for receiving the prize. She was then nominated in 1905, 1907, and 1910 by members of the legislative assembly in Portugal on the basis of her publication of the book *De la paix, du désarmement et de la solution du problème social.* No further information about her peace work activities was given by those nominating her, and I have not been able to find anything about de Weindeck in other available sources. She is truly one of the peace movement's forgotten women.

MADAME ANGELA DE OLIVEIRA CEZAR DE COSTA

Angela de Costa from Argentina was the first Latin American woman to be nominated for the Nobel Peace Prize when members of the legislative assembly in her home country launched her candidature in 1910. The parliamentarians pointed to de Costa's impressive work to prevent war between Chile and Argentina just after the turn of the century, when the relationship between the two countries was very tense. Due to her efforts, a peace treaty was negotiated and signed. Madame de Costa then started a movement to get a large peace monument erected on the border between Argentina and Chile, high up in the Andes Mountains. The statue "Christ Des Andes" was unveiled on March 13, 1904, and the president of Argentina, General Roca, paid tribute to Madame de Costa for her work for peace. Four years later, in 1908, de Costa founded "L'Association Sud Américaine de Paix Universelle." She had personally drawn up the charter of the organization, based on the principles of the Peace Society in the United States.

Anna Eckstein (1868–1947)

In 1913, for the first time, three women were nominated as Nobel Peace Prize recipients. Anna Eckstein was a newcomer, as was Lucia Ames Mead, while Hannah Priscilla Peckover had been proposed earlier. Both Lucia and Hannah were placed on the Nobel Committee's shortlist, while Anna Eckstein, in spite of her extensive work for peace over many years, received no such attention. Today, she is largely forgotten.

Anna Eckstein, the daughter of a military officer, grew up in Coburg, Germany, but moved to the United States, became an American citizen, and studied to be a teacher. She eventually became president of Boston School of Modern Languages.

As a teenager, Eckstein had met Bertha von Suttner and became very excited about her visions for a world peace movement. In America, Anna soon became an active member of the growing peace movement there. She wrote numerous articles on the requirements for the development of a peaceful international society and was also a tireless speaker at peace conventions both in the United States and Europe. From 1905 until 1911, she was vice president of the American Peace Society and played a significant role when its National Peace Congress met in Chicago in 1909.

According to Eckstein herself, her foremost contribution to the cause of peace was the large numbers of signatures she succeeded in getting to "The World Petition to Prevent War between Nations." When The Hague conference met in 1907 she had collected about two million signatures and looked forward to receiving support from participating heads of state for the principle of disarmament and resistance to militarism. But her hopes were dashed as no real support was forthcoming. The queen of the Netherlands, however, granted her an audience, and she was also invited to a meeting with the Dutch government.

Since another Hague conference was planned, Eckstein continued her efforts for peace and had managed to get as many as six million signatures to her petition when World War I broke out in 1914 and made all her work futile.

After becoming a pensioner, Anna Eckstein returned to Germany and settled in the city of her childhood, Coburg. Hitler's regime made it impossible for her to continue her peace activities, as the Nazis forbid her to speak and to publish her writings. Greatly disillusioned, she died in Coburg at the age of 79. Her nephew later donated all her manuscripts and books to the Swarthmore College Peace Collection in exchange for CARE food packages to Germany.[23]

ROSIKA SCHWIMMER (1877–1948)

In 1917, the Hungarian section of the International Committee of Women for Permanent Peace (ICWPP), nominated Rosika Schwimmer for the Nobel Peace Prize for her exceptional efforts on behalf of peace both in Europe and the United States. A generation later, in 1948, she was once again nominated, this time by, among others, illustrious Nobel laureates such as Albert Einstein and Selma Lagerlöf. In neither case did her name appear on the Nobel Committee's shortlist.

Rosika Schwimmer grew up in a Jewish middle-class family in Budapest. She did not get much formal schooling, but like so many girls from "better families" she received private education in music and languages at home. She is said to have mastered nine different languages. At the age of 18 she became occupationally active because her father's business fortunes declined. For some years she supported herself as an office worker, while she also got noticed as a journalist and public speaker.

Edith Wynner, who became Schwimmer's secretary in 1934, asserts that the adult life of the Hungarian peace activist consisted of three distinct periods. The first, the years from about age 20 to 40, was dominated by intense work for women's rights and female suffrage. With the outbreak of World War I, the second period began, dedicated to international peace work. The third period started with the communist revolution in Hungary and the civil war, which brought her career to an abrupt end. In 1921, she fled to the United States, where she spent the rest of her life.[24]

Like so many other women peace activists, Rosika Schwimmer thus came to the peace movement via the feminist movement. She started the first Hungarian labor union for women office workers and was its leader for fifteen years. In 1897, she founded the Hungarian Feminist Association and was also a cofounder of the Hungarian National Council of Women. Then, in 1913, as secretary of the International Woman Suffrage Alliance (IWSA), she went on a European speaking tour together with the American feminist Carrie Chapman Catt.

As a result of her many activities and speaking tours in Europe, Rosika Schwimmer had established an impressive network and alliances across the continent's national borders by the time the war broke out in 1914. She then decided to use her contacts to arrange peace conferences and bring the warring parties together for negotiations. Out of her own pocket she paid for the circulation of peace pamphlets in English, German, Italian, and Swedish, imploring readers to support the demand that the neutral countries must assume the mantle of leadership and appoint an arbitration conference in order to prevent an international massacre. Before the outbreak of World War I, she had managed to get an audience with the British Prime Minister David Lloyd George, to warn him about the impending danger. Lloyd George has described the meeting in his autobiography, where he notes that "such official reports as came to hand did not seem to justify the alarmist view she took of the situation."[25]

A few days after the outbreak of the war, a huge international protest demonstration, a Schwimmer initiative, was arranged; on August 4, 1914, several thousand women gathered in London. In September, she left for the United States and launched a veritable crusade to persuade Americans, and especially the women, of the need to fight against the catastrophe. Together with her friend, the prominent feminist activist Carrie Chapman Catt, she approached the secretary of state, William Jennings Bryan, who was known as an ardent devotee of peaceful arbitration. A lengthy audience with President Wilson took place shortly afterward, and Rosika presented her thoughts on how presidential leadership could contribute to a lasting peace. Then followed a half-year-long journey crisscrossing the continent giving over 400 lectures and speeches at universities, state legislative assemblies, all kinds of church denominations, ideal organizations, and, of course, women's groups. Everywhere, her message was the same: The world needs a neutral, continuous conference in order to end the present war and prevent new wars.

Thousands of press reports from Rosika Schwimmer's tour across the United States testify to her influence on public opinion. One of her fans was Henry Ford. He pledged monetary support, and, together with Rosika, he planned a neutral conference to be held in Europe, with a "Peace Ship" bringing American participants across the Atlantic. However, mighty monetary interests benefiting from the continuation of the war ridiculed the enterprise, as did the American media. Ford's expedition and the Scandinavian Line's "Oscar II," the peace ship, were presented as nothing but naïve and useless attempts by amateurs to participate in the game of international politics.

After her return to Europe, Rosika Schwimmer played a very active role in the planning and implementation of the great Women's Peace Congress that opened in The Hague in April, 1915. Over one thousand women from many countries participated, and agreed to launch the International Committee of Women for Permanent Peace, ICWPP, which in 1919 changed its name to Women's International League for Peace and Freedom, WILPF. Jane Addams and Rosika Schwimmer were elected as president and vice president of the new organization.

During the period before the United States entered the war late in 1917, Rosika Schwimmer met with President Wilson as well as with many prominent American politicians in a futile attempt to engage them in mediation talks that would put a stop to the war. She became extremely disappointed over what she perceived as vacillation and lack of determination on Wilson's part. The American president just asked the warring parties to come to him if they were interested in mediation, rather than using his power to exert active pressure in pursuit of peace. More and more, Rosika became convinced that in order to secure lasting peace, international institutions had to be established. The idea that active pacifism had to replace militarism through a system of international legal institutions suffused her thinking and activities.

When the war ended in 1918 and Hungary won its independence, the new democratic government of Prime Minister Michael Karolyi appointed Rosika Schwimmer as ambassador to Switzerland, the first female top diplomat in the world. The Swiss were shocked. That a woman, a Jew, an internationally known radical and pacifist should enter the diplomatic corps of the capital was an unbearable thought, and the authorities in Switzerland declared Rosika Schwimmer persona non grata. In spite of the protests, Rosika opened the Hungarian legation, and in the course of a few months, she managed to establish an effective administration. Civil war in Hungary, a war that ended in the Communist takeover under Bela Kun, put an stop to her diplomatic career. In 1920, she fled Hungary, and with the help of American and British Quakers, a now stateless Rosika Schwimmer set off for the United States. The third period of her life had begun, a period dominated by her work as a peace activist.

The national mood in America was now quite different from what it had been when Rosika visited the country in 1917. Schwimmer's peace activism, her pacifism, and her socialist attitudes appeared synonymous with "un-American activity" in a country where fear of communism had grown. When Rosika applied for American citizenship, it was denied on the ground that she refused to bear arms to defend the country. As the United States refused women the right to enter its military forces, this was, indeed, a most peculiar argument.

The inter-war years were difficult for Rosika Schwimmer. Her reputation as a pacifist and socialist meant that her earlier success as a writer and public speaker was compromised. Warnings against her as a "spy and a Bolshevik agent" were so effective that the person who had promoted her speaking tours earlier no longer dared to keep her on his list of clients. Newspaper editors were afraid to print her articles. Even people who believed in her idealism and integrity felt it was best to keep her at arm's length.

However, a core of faithful friends and followers remained, and in 1937, Albert Einstein, Selma Lagerlöf, and some other friends launched the "International Committee for World Peace Prize Award to Rosika Schwimmer." Their goal was to collect a sum corresponding to the size of the Nobel Peace Prize as a birthday gift to Rosika. In the introduction to the proposal, they clearly expressed their disapproval of the Norwegian Nobel Committee for not having adhered to Nobel's will:

> It was to give us pacifist leadership that Nobel founded his Peace Prize. But the several attempts to propose her name never reached the stage of actual recommendation to the Nobel Prize Committee, because her sponsors were soon warned that there was no chance for an

active, absolute pacifist like Rosika Schwimmer. If that official award cannot be anticipated, why not before it is too late make an unofficial award? All who know her brave original creative work for peace will welcome an opportunity to unite in a popular and democratic way to give Rosika Schwimmer on her sixtieth birthday, September 11, 1937, the most appropriate WORLD PEACE PRIZE.[26]

Among those supporting the initiative was New York's mayor, Fiorello H. La Guardia; the Austrian author Stefan Zweig, avid foe of Hitler and Nazism; along with several prominent Scandinavian peace activists. On December 4, 1937, twenty-two years to the day after the peace ship, "Oscar II," left for Europe, the World Peace Prize was presented to Rosika Schwimmer at a banquet held at the Waldorf-Astoria in New York. The main speech of the evening, "Unfinished Business of the Ford Expedition, World Government," was delivered by the guest of honor herself. In 1948, thirty-three parliamentarians from Great Britain, Sweden, France, Italy, and Hungary nominated Rosika Schwimmer for the Nobel Peace Prize, 31 years after she was a candidate the first time. Just like in 1917, the committee failed to place her on its shortlist. Schwimmer died in the summer of 1948. No Peace Prize was awarded that year.

MARY SHAPARD

On December 10, 1918, the very day of the Nobel Prize festivities, an American politician, Senator Morris Sheppard, sent a letter nominating Mrs. Charles R. Shapard from Texas as a candidate for the Nobel Prize. According to the senator, already in 1913, Mrs. Shapard, then known as Mary L. Christensen, had put forward plans for a "League of Nations to enforce universal peace and to reduce the enormous cost of militarism."

In his letter of nomination, Senator Sheppard also pointed out that Mary Shapard's plan

> was given wide publication and was met with universal favor. The Texas press endorsed this plan, made her an honorary member of their organization, sending the plan to President Woodrow Wilson, requesting that he make a proposal to the governments of the world to enter into a discussion for the formation of such a league.[27]

So, as long as five years before Wilson presented his famous fourteen points to the Versailles Peace Conference, including the demand for establishing a league of nations, Mary Christensen from Texas had launched the same idea. Senator Sheppard argued that simple justice demanded that she must be honored for her efforts. As he wrote:

> It now appears that such a league will be formed. I respectfully submit, therefore, that Mrs. Charles R. Shapard, formerly Mrs. Mary L. Christensen, is worthy of the Nobel Peace Prize, and I hereby nominate her for said prize.[28]

It has not been possible to find much information about Mary Shapard, nor personal data such as the dates of her birth and death. But in the archives of the Nobel Peace Institute in Oslo there is an old, yellowed newspaper clipping from 1917 that gives us a picture of the peace work Mary Shapard was engaged in over one hundred years ago. She was the leader of the Texas Federation of Women's Clubs, teachers' organizations, women's groups, and the University of Texas supported her work. "She has done more to introduce the study of the subject of peace than anyone in Texas" declares the author of the article, who adds: "It was through her influence that the Texas Legislature made May 18 Texas Peace Day, and that The

Interscholastic League of the Texas University had the subject of peace studied for two years."[29] Unfortunately, Mary Shapard's ideas did not seem to find fertile soil for growth in Texas during the past one hundred years.

MADAME SÉVERINE (1855–1929)

In 1920, a divided Nobel Committee decided to give the Peace Prize for 1919 to the American president, Woodrow Wilson, for his efforts to establish the League of Nations, an organization that his own country never joined. But, as we have already seen, it was women without formal positions in the institutional networks of power who first fought for the creation of a League of Nations. Their names are mostly forgotten today.

One of these forgotten women from the first decades of the twentieth century was a French freelance journalist known as Madame Séverine. She was nominated in 1920 by several members of the French group in the Interparliamentary Union, who regarded her as one of the foremost writers of the era: "Career: journalist, anarchist activist, editor and peace activist" is the way her biographer, Albert S. Hill, describes her in *Biographical Dictionary of Modern Peace Leaders*.[30]

The name Séverine was a pseudonym; her real name was Caroline Remy. She was born in Paris, where her father was employed as a bureaucrat. Her childhood was not a happy one, and when she was only 16 years old, Caroline married Antoine Montrobert. The marriage turned out to be very short. A later marriage to Dr. Adrian Guebhard did not last very long either, but it resulted in her also being known as "Dowager Guebhard."

Séverine was still in her twenties when she met the anarchist Jules Valles who came to influence her a great deal. She became his colleague in the magazine *Le Reveil* which he edited. In 1885, she herself became an editor of the publication *Cri du Peuple*, where she wrote numerous articles in support of striking workers and feminists. She was actively supporting the American anarchists Sacco and Vanzetti, who were unfairly condemned to death, and she also fought for the rights of poverty-stricken women in the French colonies in Africa.

By the time Séverine was nominated for the Peace Prize, she had worked as a journalist for almost four decades and could point to an enormous production of articles and books. She was from the beginning an ardent feminist, socialist, and defender of human rights, and as Albert S. Hill points out, the step from this position to the peace movement was short. She became a member of the association La Paix et le Désarmement par les Femmes and represented this organization at several national and international peace conferences.

Madame Séverine was nominated for the Nobel Peace Prize five times (1920, 1922, 1924, 1927, and 1929), but never attained the honor of being placed on the Committee's shortlist.

EGLANTYNE JEBB (1876–1928)

The same year as Madame Séverine was nominated for the Peace Prize the first time, 1920, the Red Cross International Committee proposed that the Nobel Peace Prize go to Eglantyne Jebb for her impressive work in the organization later known as Save the Children. After the end of the First World War, the allied powers had imposed trade blockades on Austria and Germany, something that led to widespread hunger among children in those countries. Eglantyne Jebb and her sister Dorothy were appalled by the extent of the misery imposed on innocent children, and in 1919, they established the "Save the Children's Fund" that raised substantial sums of money to aid children victimized by the war and the harsh policies initiated by the victors. The movement spread to other parts of the continent, and soon people all across Europe created "Save the Children" groups.

In its letter of nomination the Red Cross International Committee emphasized how Jebb had persuaded many different religious organizations, Protestants, Catholics, Orthodox, and Jews, as well as politicians from the most diverse parties, to cooperate in order to help the children who were war victims. "Yesterday's enemies, whether Germans or Frenchmen, Ottomans or Armenians, they all repeat the request, 'Save the Children,'" wrote Jebb's nominators in their letter to the Nobel Committee in 1922.[31] Huge sums of money had been donated to Save the Children, and in 1922, about 35 million Swiss francs were distributed among over thirty countries to aid children victimized by the war.

Since then, Save the Children has grown to be the largest and most respected nongovernmental organization working on behalf of children, with branches in over one hundred countries. This is the way Gro Brækken, for many years secretary general of Save the Children in Norway, described Jebb's work and personal sacrifices for the organization during its first years:

> Full of energy she launched a magnificent action to save millions of war victims, the starving and sick children on the continent. Eglantyne Jebb fought to save the enemy's children, and for this effort she was accused of treason and imprisoned.[32]

Eglantyne Jebb was born in Ellesmore in England. Her family was well off and had a strong sense of social justice that was passed on to the children. At a time when very few women received higher education, Eglantyne was admitted to Oxford University, where she studied history. Sir Richard Jebb, her uncle, was a professor at Cambridge University, and through him she made friends who would become valuable supporters of her work. She became a member of the school committee in Cambridge Village, and soon she engaged herself in charity.

Her work in this area eventually resulted in the publication of her book, *A Brief Study in Social Questions,* where she insisted that in order to be effective, charity must be based on a rational and scientific approach. Her university studies and experience with social work provided a solid foundation for the development of the organization that would become her legacy to the world.

Eglantyne Jebb soon established herself as the undisputed leader of Save the Children, soliciting the aid of the pope and other religious leaders for her work. She also approached political parties both in Great Britain and other countries requesting support. Under her leadership, Save the Children extended its work to include children in parts of the world other than Western Europe. Thus, when a catastrophic famine hit the Soviet Union during the 1920s, Save the Children came to the rescue.

Besides attention to practical matters to alleviate the horrors caused by war, Jebb started work on the draft of an international treaty to recognize children's rights. She was the author of what became known as The Geneva Declaration of the Rights of the Child, adopted by the League of Nations in 1924, and forerunner of the United Nations' Convention of the Rights of the Child, which has now been ratified by almost all countries in the world. Today, a century after she began her work, children are reaping the rewards of her efforts on behalf of youngsters everywhere.

ELSA BRÄNDSTRÖM (1888–1948)

Sweden's Elsa Brändström was the only woman from one of the Nordic countries to be nominated for the Nobel Peace Prize during the period from 1901 to 1960. Her immense effort to help the victims of the First World War lay behind her nomination in 1928.

Brändström was born in St. Petersburg, where her father

was a military delegate, but she grew up in Sweden. When she was twenty years old she returned to Russia. Her father was now a member of the diplomatic corps, and through him Elsa gained access to Russia's most exclusive social circles. When the war broke out in 1914, she immediately signed up for a Red Cross nursing education course in order to be able to help war victims. Because of her father's position, she soon became aware of the fate of prisoners of war and the diplomatic discussions about their captivity. In the fall of 1914, she started visiting the camps for prisoners of war, a practice she continued for the duration of the war. Due to her father's influence, she was able to get many prisoners released and returned to their home countries.

After the signing of the Brest-Litovsk peace treaty, Elsa Brändström continued her active work for the war prisoners, and, from 1918 to 1920, she worked in Siberia, tending sick prisoners who had not yet been released. In an open letter to the International Red Cross she begged the organization to help get more of these prisoners returned to their own countries, at the same time describing the horrible situation in the camps: "The war prisoner in Russia is outside the law. He enjoys no rights and has no protection." She reports visiting a camp where only five of 600 prisoners survived and another with 5,000 survivors among a camp population of 17,000. Her conclusion: "The desperate cries of the dead and the dying will never reach the door of the world outside."[33]

Elsa Brändström's efforts made sure that the "desperate cries" of the prisoners of war were finally heard by the rest of the world. Her book about her experiences, *Bland Krigsfångar: Ryssland och Siberien* (Among Prisoners of War: Russia and Siberia), was reissued several times, and all the proceeds went toward the building of rehabilitation hospitals for war veterans. The book made a deep impression on the Nobel Committee's consultant, Wilhelm Keilhau, who described it as one of the most memorable documents about the war. He was also effusive in his praise of Elsa. In his summary to the Nobel Committee, he mentioned her intense feeling of duty toward those suffering hardship and her incessant work to realize "this self-imposed duty." He concluded: "She is definitely one of the noblest figures among those who during the dark years of the world war dared to oppose the military brutality with her own love."[34]

Elsa Brändström received a great deal of honor for her work. The war veterans loved "die Elsa," and she was awarded honorary doctorates at the universities of Königsberg and Uppsala. But the Nobel Prize eluded her. Overlooking Keilhau's good recommendation, the Nobel Committee decided not to award any prize in 1928, in spite of having two outstanding women, Elsa Brändström and Jane Addams, on its list of nominees.

LADY ABERDEEN (1854–1939)

Ishbel Maria Marjorbanks was born into the British aristocracy as the daughter of Lord Tweedmouth. After her marriage to Lord Aberdeen, an active politician in Great Britain's Liberal Party, she became known as Lady Aberdeen. She developed a strong social conscience and used her position in her class-divided society to organize reform movements to benefit those less fortunate than herself. She was particularly concerned about the situation of working-class women and supported William Gladstone and his Strand Rescue Mission. She also founded organizations herself to further women's interests.

As her position within the feminist movement grew, she received international attention, and in 1893, she was elected as president of the International Council of Women (ICW). With some short breaks, she retained this position until the middle of the 1930s. But her Curriculum Vitae did not impress the Nobel Committee's consultant when Lady Aberdeen was nominated the first time in 1931. In a rather condescending fashion he points out that the nominations of Lady Aberdeen "all emanate from women," and that the initiative evidently comes from "some women's council, most likely the Danish one," since the most detailed reasoning in support of the nomination was written by a well-known Danish feminist.[35] He further notes that Lady Aberdeen's work for peace has manifested itself only through her role in the International Council of Women, where she "has had valuable help, and during the last few years has served more as the Council's figurative leader than its soul."[36] In the same condescending tone he insinuates that it most likely was Lady Aberdeen's aristocratic position through birth and marriage, not her personal ability that secured her election as leader of the ICW. His conclusive remark to the committee: "I have met Lady Aberdeen…in Oslo and had a lengthy conversation with her. She appears kind and sweet-tempered, but rather insignificant."[37]

Lady Aberdeen was nominated for the Peace Prize a total of six times between 1931 and 1937. Several of the nominations were made by Nordic female parliamentarians, who appear not to have shared the opinions uttered by the Nobel Committee's consultant. In the nominating letter of 1935 they acknowledge the contribution to peace made by the ICW and write that it was Lady Aberdeen who "to a very large degree" deserved credit for this work.[38] The parliamentarians also emphasized that during the war the organizational structure of the ICW remained intact, "not least due to Lady Aberdeen's personal influence."[39] When Lady Aberdeen was nominated for the last time in 1937, the Canadian Prime minister, MacKenzie King was one of her staunch supporters. Lady Aberdeen was popular in Canada, where she had been a very active First Lady while her husband was Governor General toward the end of the nineteenth century. It was due to her initiative that the National Council of Women of Canada was established. Regarding her role in the International Council of Women, MacKenzie King stated the following in his letter of nomination:

> So considerable has been the part played by Lady
> Aberdeen in the work of The International Council of
> Women that her name has become identified with that
> organization, almost to the exclusion of every other
> name.[40]

Today, her name, along with so many of the other women
nominees of the period, is forgotten by most.

ANNIE BESANT (1847–1933)

In 1931, there were three women nominees for the Peace
Prize: Jane Addams, who became a prize winner at last, and
two newcomers, Lady Aberdeen and Annie Besant. Unlike Jane
Addams and Lady Aberdeen, Annie Besant (née Wood) came
from a modest middle-class English background. Only 20 years
old, she married Frank Besant, a clergyman in the Church of
England. It was a mismatched union—he a conservative Tory,
she a feminist and socialist activist. They were legally separated
in 1873, but never obtained a divorce. Frank Besant got full cus-
tody of the two small children, as the court considered Annie,
with her radical views, unable to give them a good upbringing.

During the following decades, Annie Besant became a
prolific author and supporter of women's rights, the rights of
workers to unionize, and the struggle for independence in
Ireland and India. She joined the National Secular Society and
was soon one of its leading spokespersons. As a member of the
Marxist Social Democratic Federation and the Fabian Society,
she also gained attention as an excellent public speaker.

Waning interests in secular matters made Annie Besant
turn to the Theosophical Society, and she eventually became
its international leader. As the headquarters of the society was
in India, she moved there and became a member of the Indian

National Congress party, where she rose to become leader in 1917.

Not surprisingly, Annie Besant earned a reputation as a rebel and revolutionary socialist, but the Nobel Committee consultant, Ragnvald Moe, in his evaluation of her candidacy reassured the Committee members that her revolutionary rhetoric was quite harmless: "There is not any evidence of a revolutionary bent in her contribution to Shaw's well-known essay collection *Fabian Essays on Socialism*." On the contrary, incremental reform was, according to him, Besant's preferred way to a more peaceful world. Her writings were more literary than "thoroughly reasoned and based on solid social studies," but he conceded that Besant was a great speaker with "rare gifts for public performance and definite organizational talents."

Moe also praised Besant as a "brave and free spirit" who in spite of "an often eccentric appearance time and again proves herself to be an English realist in her politics."[41] Ragnvald Moe recognized Annie Besant's influence on the development of Indian nationalist consciousness. She has, says he, "maybe stronger than any native Indian, placed herself squarely on nationalistic grounds." Her publication, *New India,* was the most important organ of the National Congress party, and her articles completely dismissed the legitimacy of British rule in India, demanding "Home Rule" for the country.[42] In Great Britain, Annie Besant's influence on Indian politics was regarded with great scepticism by the politicians. To them, she was a demagogue and a renegade, and in 1917, she was imprisoned by the British authorities in India. She was, however, let go after a short time, and later the same year she was elected as leader of the National Congress.

It was the British parliamentarian Peter Freeman who had proposed Annie Besant as a candidate for the Nobel Prize, citing her persistent work for understanding between East and West as a valuable contribution to the cause of international peace. Moe made it quite clear that he did not share Freeman's views. "Annie Besant has not in the course of her long life worked as a dedicated friend of peace," he states, since she "first and foremost wants to build peace on social justice." Further, from the English point of view, "she is understandably regarded as a trouble maker."[43] Since Besant's work was considered provocative, she was, by implication, not relevant as a Peace Prize recipient. Moe also maintains that her role in Indian politics was exaggerated, for, says he, "if one reads through the professional political literature, it is clear that the authors don't pay much attention to her."[44]

Moe's objections to Besant's candidacy illustrate how the attitudes toward potential Peace Prize laureates have changed. Many of the Prize recipients during more recent decades have certainly been regarded as "trouble makers" in their own countries as well as in large parts of the world. Being the subject of discussion in "professional literature" is not necessarily a good indicator when it comes to predicting the winner of the Peace Prize.

Possibly, however, it was not so much Moe's opinion of Besant's politics that determined his position in this matter, but rather his view of India's colonial relationship to Great Britain. In the concluding remarks of his summary to the Nobel Committee, he states that he felt obliged to "join the many professional experts who contend that India is not yet mature enough to become a self-ruling British dominion."[45] Perhaps it was apprehension about the Committee offending a world power, rather than his personal opinion of Annie Besant that dictated his advice to the Nobel Committee members.

PRINCESS MARGUERITE-ANTONETTE HERACLIUS DJABADARY

The only woman nominated for the Nobel Peace Prize in 1933 was originally from Georgia in the Soviet Union. It was the French professor of international law and member of the Institute of International Law, Charles Dupuis, who, in a very short letter to the Nobel Committee proposed Princess Marguerite-Antoinette as a Peace Prize candidate because she had written the libretto of the opera "Goulnara." The music was composed by her husband, Heraclius Djabadary. Professor Dupuis felt strongly that the opera represented "the ideal of peace" and that "as a piece of art it would serve the cause of peace through a genuine voice, something which never, as far as I know, has happened earlier."[46] Due to lack of finances, the opera had never been performed, and Professor Dupuis wished the Nobel Committee to step in as sponsor.

I have not been able to find any more information about the princess. Her husband, however, is briefly presented by Wikipedia as the composer of the opera "Goulnara." He was born in 1891 and died in Nice on August 19, 1937. His wife is not mentioned at all as the librettist.

JANET MILLER (1873–1958)

Janet Miller, candidate for the Nobel Peace Prize in 1935, was from Nashville, Tennessee. Her father, Dr. Wesley Miller, a physician, left his profession to study theology, and later he became a minister and missionary in the Methodist Church. The daughter eventually followed in her father's footsteps, going to Japan as a missionary for the Southern Methodist Church and teaching at a girls' school in Hiroshima for several years before she started medical studies and eventually became an eye surgeon. As a missionary and physician, she worked both in Japan and China before she ended up as director of Margaret Williamson Maternity Hospital in Shanghai, the very first mother-and-child hospital in the city. Along with her work as a doctor, she was also a music teacher and spent much of her time helping blind children read and write. She worked for a shorter period as a missionary doctor both in the Belgian Congo and the Middle East before returning to the United States where she gained popularity as a writer and public speaker.

All the people behind Janet Miller's nomination mentioned the profound influence she had exercised through her health-and-humanitarian work, breaking down both racial and national barriers. Two members of the Japanese legislature, Joichi Yamaji and Goro Arakawa, described her as "the most powerful factor for international friendships and mutual understandings between nations in the world today," a person who had especially contributed to the understanding of Japan and its people in the West. Nathan L. Bachman, a U. S. senator, chose to focus on her work among international students. Through a couple of decades Miller had conducted regular meetings with students in the cities where she worked: New York, Chicago, Paris, London, and Shanghai. In Paris, a couple of dozen nations were represented at her weekly sessions. Senator Bachman underlined Dr. Miller's influence through these small "peace conferences" she had organized over so many years in different parts of the world and argued that when people are inspired by an idea, their power and influence will be widely felt.[47]

JULIE BIKLE (1871–1962)

In 1935, Julie Bikle from Winterthur, Switzerland was nominated for the Nobel Peace Prize. The proposals stressed her unselfish work on behalf of all the Germans victimized by World War I, families who had lost contact with each other and the many prisoners of war. The people behind her candidacy pointed in particular to her impressive effort to help the children who had suffered so much because of the war. She had raised vast sums of money to support German children and pay for their education. Food and clothing were collected in order to combat the worst effects of the war, and through her efforts more than 50,000 underfed and sick children, many of whom were ill with tuberculosis, received medical care in Switzerland, regained their health, and got a new start in life.

One of Bikle's nominators, Dr. Emil Abderhalden, wrote this strong recommendation, which probably sounded better in 1935 than it does today:

> Es ist charakteristisch für die gewaltige, selbstlose Leistung von Fraulein Bikle, dass sie vielfach für einen Mann gehalten wurde. Die Überraschung war immer gross, wenn bekannt wurde, dass eine Frau ohne jede Unterstützung ganz von sich ein so gewaltiges, die Welt umspannendes Werk aufgebaut habe. (It is characteristic of the immense, unselfish effort of Ms. Bikle that she is often believed to be a man. The surprise was always great when it became known that a woman without any support had built up such an impressive, worldwide enterprise completely on her own).[48]

Julie Bikle was nominated two more times, both in 1936 and 1937, but never gained a place on the Nobel Committee's shortlist.

MOINA BELLE MICHAEL (1869–1944)

For the first time in the history of the Nobel Peace Prize, as many as four women were nominated in 1936. Moina Belle Michael was one of the four. After the end of World War I she had launched the idea of adopting the poppy as a symbol honoring fallen soldiers. The American Legion, one of the veterans' organizations in the United States, became excited about her proposal, and, in 1920, chose the poppy as its memorial flower. Since then, the sale of these small silk blossoms has produced considerable amounts of money every year, money which in turn goes to the survivors of fallen soldiers or to injured veterans and their relatives.

Moina Belle Michael was born in the vicinity of the little town of Good Hope in the state of Georgia. Her father, John Marion Michael, had fought on the side of the Confederacy in the Civil War and had participated in some of the bloodiest and most decisive battles. Her mother, Alice Sherwood Wise, came from one of Virginia's prominent families, and Moina's upbringing was heavily influenced by the conservative, religious environment in the rural South.

Moina Belle Michael started her career as a teacher as a young teenager. She was only 15 years old when she got her first job teaching at a small rural school. She received her teacher's degree in her home state of Georgia and later studied at Columbia University. Eventually, she became a professor at the University of Georgia and was one of the most respected pedagogues in the United States when she retired in 1938, after a more than 50-year-long teaching career. By then, she was also known as the "Poppy Lady" in many countries.

The story of how her "poppy project" got started is rather moving and deserves recounting. Just a couple of days before the end of World War I, Moina, quite by chance, picked up a copy of the magazine *Ladies Home Journal* and read the poem "In Flanders Fields" about the poppies blooming on the graves of fallen soldiers.

In Flanders fields the poppies blow
  Between the crosses row on row,
  That mark our place; and in the sky
  The larks, still bravely singing, fly.
  Scarce heard amid the guns below.

We are the Dead. Short days ago
  We lived, felt dawn, saw sunset glow,
  Loved and were loved, and now we lie

47

In Flanders fields.

Take up our quarrel with the foe:
   To you from failing hands we throw
   The torch; be yours to hold it high.
   If ye break faith with us who die
   We shall not sleep, though poppies grow
   In Flanders fields.

Deeply moved by the poem, Moina decided to organize the production and sale of artificial poppies in order to raise money for veterans of war and their families. The campaign caught on and spread from the United States to England and France and more than fifty other countries. The tradition is still alive, and during the 2014 ceremonies marking the invasion of France seventy years earlier, many of the participants were seen wearing the little silk flowers.

It was Dr. Cullen B. Gosnell, professor of political science at Emory University, who nominated Moina Michael as a candidate for the Nobel Peace Prize. In his letter of nomination he referred to the huge sums of money for the support of war veterans and their families that the poppy campaigns had produced, arguing that nobody had done these groups a greater favor than Moina Michael. Four years after her death, the postal service in the United States issued a stamp in her memory.

IRMA SCHWEITZER (1882–1967)*

Both in 1936 and 1937, Dr. N.A. Nilsson from Örebro in Sweden proposed Irma Schweitzer as a Nobel Peace Prize candidate. His letters to the Nobel Committee were very scanty; he did not even include the date of her birth. He did, however, inform the Committee that she was from Metz in France and the author of a book entitled *Sur le chemin de la paix*. Fortunately, an obituary written by Jacques Kaspar a year after Schweitzer's death[49] gives information that makes it possible to present a clearer picture of her. The short article by Mr. Kaspar reveals Schweitzer as an important figure within the European peace movement during the period between the two world wars and, indeed, for some time after the end of World War II. She certainly deserves to be remembered instead of shrouded in forgetfulness.

Irma Schweitzer was born in Baden, Germany, one of the seven children of Moritz and Sara Meyer. After completing elementary schooling in Baden, her Jewish parents sent her to a boarding school in Lausanne for further education. Following her marriage to the chemical engineer Etienne Schweitzer from Metz, she rarely visited Baden. The couple settled in Metz and became active participants in humanitarian work. They joined several national and international organizations (religious, secular, and pacifist), which they also supported financially, as well as serving on the executive boards of various institutions. As a result of her social and humanitarian involvement, Irma Schweitzer developed an extensive international network and was acquainted with political and cultural personalities from many parts of the world, among them Eleanor Roosevelt, Winston Churchill, and Albert Schweitzer, to name just a few. She received many prizes for her work as a peace activist, both from veterans' organizations and Red Cross societies.

In addition to being organizationally active, Irma Schweitzer was a frequent contributor to journals and the opinion pages of newspapers, as well as a novelist and poet. Andre Maurois wrote the preface to her deeply moving poetry collection *Lueur dans les Tenebres,* which was published in 1947, inspired particularly by the Jews' sufferings under the Holocaust.

Concluding his remarks about Irma Schweitzer, Jacques Kaspar compares her contribution to the peace movement to that of Bertha von Suttner. Ironically, Schweitzer is one of the Nobel Peace Prize candidates the world has almost totally forgotten.

*Also known as Irma Schweitzer-Meyer

HENRIETTA SZOLD (1860–1945)

Four women were among the candidates nominated for the Peace Prize in 1937. In addition to Lady Aberdeen, Julie Bikle, and Irma Schweitzer, who had all been proposed before, there was a newcomer, the American philanthropist Henrietta Szold. She was nominated by Senator Royal S. Copeland and warmly supported by the governor of New York, Herbert Lehman.

Henrietta Szold was from Baltimore, Maryland. Her father was a well-known rabbi in the city, and Szold received a solid education in general studies and Hebrew. Her goal was to become a teacher, but as she learned about the pogroms against Jews in Russia at the end of the nineteenth century as well as their difficult situation in many other countries, she decided that her task in life would be that of a bridge builder between Jews and other people in their various homelands. Szold became a pioneer in the United States in the area of adult education and rapid integration of immigrants. Through translation, editing, and publication of Jewish writings, she also conveyed knowledge of important parts of Jewish culture to American readers.

Henrietta Szold was an early convert to the Zionist idea of a homeland for Jews in Palestine. She became one of the founders of Hadassah, the American Zionist organization's female branch. In 1937, the same year that Szold was a candidate for the Nobel Peace Prize, Hadassah had about 60,000 members and several times more supporters. One of Hadassah's projects was to make modern health services accessible to the people of Palestine, and the organization built an impressive number of hospitals and clinics in the area, as well as the first nursing school in Palestine. The services these institutions offered were accessible to all, regardless of race or religion—Christians, Muslims, and Jews were all welcome, no one was excluded.

Between 1922 and 1937, Henrietta Szold lived and worked

in Palestine. She was for some time the director of Jewish education and worked to help Jewish immigrants. After Hitler came to power in Germany in 1933, she took on the responsibility of helping to get thousands of Jewish children admitted to Palestine, thus undoubtedly saving their lives.

"No other woman in America is more respected," wrote Senator Copeland in his letter to the Norwegian Nobel Committee when nominating her for the Peace Prize in 1937. Governor Herbert Lehman of New York was no less effusive in his praise:

> Miss Szold has cut across national boundaries and helped dissolve national animosities. She has shown how to enrich the new homelands of émigrés with cultural and human values. She has undertaken a constructive and peaceful solution of one of the most grievous and disturbing problems of our time, the persecution, expatriation, and homelessness of a large number of Jews.[50]

Underlying all of Henrietta Szold's work in Palestine was a firm conviction that a future independent state must be a binational state of both Arabs and Jews, living as equals in a developed welfare society. Tragically, the infrastructure of a modern medical system and health institutions that she created and which should eventually have become the base of Israel's health service, is now largely benefiting just one of the peoples she dedicated her life to help.

PRINCESS HENRIETTE OF BELGIUM (1870–1948)

In 1938, once more, there was only one woman nominated for the Nobel Peace Prize, namely Princess Henriette of Belgium. She was proposed as a candidate by a member of the French Senate, Marquis de Juigne. But his letter of nomination was very short. He mentioned that the princess had "dedicated all of her life to good deeds, in order to lighten the pains of the suffering, having transformed her house and palace to hospitals and altered women's clothing to be used by the Red Cross to make bandages for the wounded." Thus, the princess had experienced the war herself and "completely dedicated herself to the work of peace." The Marquis de Juigne also pointed to her royal background; her husband was the descendant of the French King Louis-Philippe and Queen Amélie. Princess Henriette was also the aunt of Belgium's King Leopold III and had used her royal status to work for peace.[51]

CARRIE CHAPMAN CATT (1859–1947)

World War II broke out in 1939, and no Peace Prize awards were made that year. However, all together twenty people were nominated, among them President Roosevelt, the British Prime Minister, Neville Chamberlain, and Adolf Hitler. (The nomination of Hitler was submitted by the Swedish parliamentarian, E.G.C. Brandt, but was later withdrawn. As a curiosity, one may also mention that Italy's dictator, Benito Mussolini, had been nominated in 1935).

The lone woman among the candidates in 1939 was the American feminist leader, Carrie Chapman Catt, whose nomination was proposed by two professors from Columbia University. Carrie Chapman Catt grew up in Wisconsin, United States. When she was nominated for the Peace Prize, she had been fighting for women's rights for decades and was known not only in the United States but internationally as a feminist, pacifist, and peace activist. She paid her way through Iowa State College by working as a teacher while studying, since her father refused to spend money on educating a girl. But Carrie's career as a teacher was relatively short. In 1885 she married Leo Chapman, the editor of an Iowa newspaper, and worked as a journalist in his paper. Chapman died just a year after the wedding, and Carrie then moved to San Francisco, where she continued to work as a journalist. Shortly, however, she returned to Iowa and married George Catt, a wealthy engineer who shared her political ideas and joined her in her fight for women's rights.

Carrie Chapman Catt soon became a leading figure in the American struggle for women's voting rights. When Susan B. Anthony retired in 1900 as president of the National American Woman Suffrage Association (NAWSA), Carrie Chapman Catt became her successor. Four years later she was elected president of the International Woman Suffrage Alliance, a position she kept until 1923. The job offered her important opportunities to travel and become intimately acquainted with women's conditions in all parts of the world and to develop her leadership talents to the fullest. When she was nominated for the Nobel Peace Prize in 1939, Wilhelm Keilhau, the consultant to the Nobel Committee, declared in his evaluation of her candidacy that the International Woman Suffrage Alliance was "surely the best organized and hardest working women's organization that world history up to this time has seen,"[52] and he ascribed this fact particularly to Catt's talents as an administrator.

Carrie Chapman Catt was not only a great organizational talent, but also an impressive public speaker, with an outgoing, warm personality. Keilhau gives this description of her:

> In common with other organizers of world dimensions, she has an impressive memory. Besides this, she is a great orator. I don't know anyone that I will place ahead of her in this regard, even though I have heard both Bjørnson and Lloyd George.[53]

The initiative to honor Carrie Chapman Catt with a Peace Prize nomination originated on the American East coast, where two women of Norwegian ancestry, Maria Bang Hansen and Magnhild Schou, headed a committee to work for her candidacy. They contacted Columbia University and persuaded two professors there to send a formal nomination to the Nobel Committee. No reasoned argument for the nomination was submitted. This was, according to Keilhau, not at all surprising: "For in the United States the name Carrie Chapman Catt is so well known that for an American it has surely appeared sufficient only to mention it."[54]

For the international feminist movement it was, of course, an enormous asset to have a leader like Carrie Chapman Catt. Through her frequent travels she gained important insight in both national and international problems. Her travels also made her increasingly concerned about threats to peace and positive to the emerging peace movement. Wherever she travelled, reports Keilhau, she insisted on meeting leaders from different parties and political environments, listening to their analysis of the conflicts that existed. For, as he writes:

> Precisely because she always recognized the relativity of things, she became convinced that when differing opinions could be expressed in a peaceful, democratic meeting of minds, over the course of time it would be possible to arrive at rational solutions of existing historical problems.[55]

Carrie Chapman Catt was firmly convinced that feminism and peace activism were closely intertwined and that if women gained equal access to political participation, war would be impossible. "Mrs. Catt assumed that as a friend of peace she was acting on the most important of all work arenas when she labored for female suffrage,"[56] says Keilhau.

After the outbreak of war in 1914, Carrie Chapman Catt dedicated herself more and more to organized peace work. During the inter-war period, when differences arose between the absolute pacifists, who under no circumstances would tolerate a resort to arms, and those believing it was necessary to be prepared to confront totalitarianism, Catt supported the latter view, and believed in the legitimacy of military opposition to fascism and Nazi dictatorships. However, she also spoke out forcefully against the results of anticommunist hysteria in the United States, which she held to be inconsistent with the constitutional rights of citizens in a democratic state.

Carrie Chapman Catt was a good friend of many politicians, among them Franklin Delano Roosevelt and Woodrow Wilson, but refrained from engaging in party politics because of her position as a peace and women's activist. She therefore also refused to be nominated for a seat in the American Congress. However, she cooperated closely with Eleanor Roosevelt, both as a feminist and as a peace activist.

In spite of Wilhelm Keilhau's admiration for Catt, he did not advise the Nobel Committee to honor her with the Peace Prize. In his remarks to the Committee he writes:

If women had succeeded, through their participation in the political life of our time, to avert international tensions and the Second World War, then Carrie Chapman Catt, as the dominant leader of the suffrage movement, would have been one of the strongest leaders ever suggested for the Peace Prize.[57]

And he concludes:

Now her candidature is shadowed by a world historical problem, which surely will give future historians much to ponder: What is the fundamental cause why female suffrage and totalitarian militarism have been victorious during the same time period.[58]

This coupling of women's rights and totalitarianism is indeed peculiar. Far from having succeeded in arriving at any breakthrough for their cause during the inter-war period, women were still without political influence in practically all countries. In spite of having attained the suffrage in some western nations, in no state were they admitted to the decision-making forums in such numbers that they could exercise real political influence. No Peace Prize was awarded in 1939. Once more, an obviously qualified woman was passed over.

CHAPTER 3
THE POSTWAR PERIOD 1945–1960

During the Second World War no Nobel Peace Prize was awarded, and among the few nominations arriving at the Nobel Institute in Oslo between 1939 and 1945, there were no women. When the Committee met in 1945, it decided to give the prize for 1944 to the International Committee of the Red Cross, and the prize for 1945 was given to the American Secretary of State, Cordell Hull.

During the period from 1946 to 1950, seven women were nominated for the Peace Prize, namely, Emily Greene Balch from the United States, Alexandra Kollontay from the Soviet Union, Eleanor Roosevelt, Britain's Katharine Bruce Glasier, Rosika Schwimmer from Hungary (also nominated in 1917), the internationally known pedagogue Maria Montessori from Italy, and Peruvian Eva Peron, together with her husband, president Juan Peron.

Three of these women were placed on the shortlist, but only one of them became a Nobel Laureate, namely Emily Greene Balch. The two others, Eleanor Roosevelt and Alexandra Kollontay were, in spite of impressive credentials, not found worthy of the honor.

From 1951 to 1960, yet another seven women were nominated for the Nobel Peace Prize, none of them, however, obtained the prize. Among the men nominated during the same years were the dictators Josef Stalin and Juan Peron, as well as Mahatma Gandhi, who in spite of large support and many nominations, was passed over by the Nobel Committee, maybe out of reluctance to offend the British.

EMILY GREENE BALCH (1867–1961)

The third woman awarded the Nobel Peace Prize was Emily Greene Balch, the undisputed leader of Women's International League for Peace and Freedom (WILPF), which will be discussed below. Greene Balch grew up in Boston, Massachusetts, the daughter of a lawyer. Her family was very wealthy, and she received an extremely good education, first at private schools and then at the prestigious Bryn Mawr College, where she graduated in 1889. The following two years she studied sociology and economics in Paris. Later, she pursued studies at Harvard and the University of Chicago, before spending the 1895–96 academic year as an economics student in Berlin. It was, therefore, a uniquely qualified young woman who was appointed in 1896 to a teaching position at Wellesley College. Emily remained there for twenty years, lecturing on subjects like social economics, statistics, and the history of socialism and the labor union movement.

Besides her academic career, Balch also spent much time during these years as a volunteer doing practical social work. The outbreak of World War I caused her to dedicate the rest of her life to peace work. Feminism and peace activism were intertwined according to Balch, and in 1916 she applied for, and was granted, two years leave of absence from her position as professor at Wellesley, in order to spend her full time as a peace worker through the International Committee of Women for Permanent Peace, (ICWPP), later known as WILPF. This in fact ended her academic career; in 1918, she was unceremoniously fired from Wellesley. After America entered the war, there was no tolerance for the uncompromising pacifism that Emily professed. Finn Seyersted, the consultant who evaluated her candidacy, notes in his report to the Committee that Professor Randall, who nominated Greene Balch for the Nobel Peace Prize in 1946, had commented in his letter of nomination that her dismissal from Wellesley was due to "her work for peace and her outspoken pacifism in combination with her radical socioeconomic views that were too difficult for the leadership to digest."[1]

Emily Greene Balch had been a very active participant in the famous international women's congress that met in The Hague in 1915. The congress adopted a detailed program for peace that included many of the fourteen points submitted by President Wilson to the peace conference in Versailles and for which he won international acclaim and the Nobel Peace Prize in 1919. But when a delegation of women presented their plan to the president in 1915, Wilson refused to accept their advice to initiate a conciliation conference between the warring nations. As Seyersted notes, the president examined the women's congress proposals "very closely," and the fourteen points that he later submitted as his own "included to a great extent the same concrete proposals as the Hague Congress had launched."[2]

The Hague Congress dispatched delegations of women to several European countries in the spring of 1915 in order to influence politicians to assume the mantle of leadership for peace. Emily Greene Balch participated in a delegation sent to Oslo, Norway. The women were granted audiences with King Haakon VII, the Prime Minister, and the Secretary of State, and also met with the leadership of the Storting, the Norwegian national legislature. Christian L. Lange, the Secretary General of the Inter-parliamentary Union and previous secretary of the Norwegian Nobel Committee, also received Greene Balch and her fellow delegates at the Nobel Institute. Wherever they went, whether to warring or neutral countries, the women experienced understanding and goodwill. But no concrete results of their efforts materialized.

Actually, this should not be a surprise to anyone. Women were not represented in the decision-making forums at the national level, as only Australia, New Zealand, Norway, and Finland had granted women the right to vote in national elections. Without political influence, women's means to have any effect on the international situation was naturally severely limited. Therefore, one of the demands of the Hague Congress was precisely that universal suffrage on equal terms for men and women must be adopted as a human right.

Nonetheless, Finn Seyersted praised the female peace activists for their work, stating in his evaluation of Emily Greene Balch: "There was hardly any other numerous group within the warring countries, the Socialist parties included, which to the same extent managed to put aside national differences and agree on a just and practical program for peace."[3]

As already mentioned, at the end of World War I, Emily Greene Balch faced unemployment. She worked for a short time in the editorial offices of *The Nation* in New York, but after 1919 her major preoccupation was feminism and peace activism. During the entire inter-war period she was one of the most prominent members of WILPF, traveling extensively on behalf of the organization. She spent time in the Middle East, meeting with both Jewish and Arab leaders, as well as the British governing authorities of Palestine. She was critical of Zionism, advocating constructive reforms that would be in the interest of both Jews and Muslims. After Hitler's victory in Germany in 1933, she made a formidable effort to aid European refugees, in particular the Jews. Both in her public appearances and essays she argued forcefully that European refugees constituted a valuable resource for the countries willing to accept them. One of her brochures, "To our Jewish Fellow Sufferers," was written as a personal letter and distributed to about 50,000 influential Americans. Altogether, according to Seyersted, she contributed greatly to Americans altering their attitudes to immigration from Europe at a time when that continent was threatened by war. She was also very critical of the United States interment of its citizens with Japanese backgrounds in 1942 and made substantial efforts to aid this group of Americans both during and after the war.

Emily Greene Balch was a Quaker, but when Pearl Harbor was attacked in 1941, she considered military defense to be the right response. Passive response, or nonviolent resistance on the model of Gandhi, was not possible in this situation, she maintained. Still, many Americans considered even this moderate form of pacifism to be unpatriotic, and when Emily was awarded the Nobel Prize for 1946, it was not met with enthusiasm in the United States. President Harry Truman was among the critics of the Nobel Committee's decision. It is testimony not only to his poor judgment, but also his incredible pettiness, that he not only abstained from sending the customary congratulatory telegram to the Nobel laureate, but also failed to invite her to the White House banquet he threw for her fellow winner, John Mott.

Emily Greene Balch was often unfavorably compared to her good friend and colleague through many decades, Jane Addams. Seyersted, however, is of the opinion that while Addams possibly had more influence on the average American man or woman, Balch might have "exercised more direct influence on authorities in decision-making positions."[4] He also asserts that as Addams' successor and the undisputed leader of the international peace movement, Balch had, to a far greater extent than Addams, put other things aside in order to dedicate herself to the cause of peace.

Obtaining the Nobel Peace Prize did not make Emily

Greene Balch more popular among her country men. In her article "Jane Addams and Emily Greene Balch: The Two Women of WILPF," Harriet Hyman Alonso points to conventional gender role patterns to explain this:

> For women, working with the poor, the ill, or the homeless is acceptable and even honorable. Working on the international level, especially as regarding diplomatic affairs, is inappropriate and, at times, treasonous. In this sense, the theory of 'separate spheres' holds true. Jane Addams is remembered for her "woman's work," whereas Emily Greene Balch is virtually ignored because she crossed the line of appropriate female behavior in the public sphere.[5]

ALEXANDRA KOLLONTAY (1872–1952)

The same year that Emily Greene Balch received the Nobel Peace Prize, the Soviet Union's Alexandra Kollontay was also nominated. Twenty-three Norwegian parliamentarians from the Labor Party and the Norwegian Communist Party stood behind the nomination. The Finnish government led by Prime Minister Paasikivi as well as members of the Finnish parliament had also sent in nominations that were supported by several women's associations in both Norway and Sweden.

It was first and foremost Kollontay's untiring efforts as a peace mediator between Finland and the Soviet Union that were emphasized by those proposing her name. Thus, the Norwegian nomination underscored her "important, maybe decisive effort to solve the conflicts between Finland and the Soviet Union."[6]

Alexandra Kollontay was born in St. Petersburg, the daughter of a well-to-do family belonging to the Russian nobility. Her mother was Finnish, but both the Finnish grandparents were dead when she was born. However, their home in Karelen, near Viborg, was Alexandra's childhood summer paradise. There she acquired knowledge of Finnish culture and formed close friendships.

More than anyone else, it was Alexandra's father General Michail Domontovich, who helped shape her character from a very early age. Regarding his importance in her life, she writes: "If ever a man has influenced my development, it is my father," and adds that he admired Voltaire and "poked fun of those who judged people because of their rank and descent. He believed in liberalism."[7] During her early years, Alexandra became acquainted with Darwin's theory of evolution and John Stuart Mill's liberal writings. Maria Strachova, Alexandra's private tutor, was another important figure during her upbringing. Jens Arup Seip, the Nobel Committee consultant, writes that Strachova had a reputation as a dangerous nihilist, while she in fact was just "a cautious oppositionist" who did not get involved in political actions, but tried simply to spread knowledge among the common folk.[8] Through Maria Strachova, Alexandra got involved in social work and adult education for Russian workers. This in turn led to contact with people oriented toward more leftist views.

In 1898, Alexandra went to Switzerland to study. Her return to Russia was via Finland, where she met the founder of the Finnish labor movement, Nils of Ursin, who just then was leading a huge strike by textile workers. Jens Arup Seip reports that the first task Alexandra turned to when arriving in Russia was "to organize a movement of economic support for the Finns."[9]

From now on, Alexandra Kollontay was actively involved in illegal work against the tsarist regime. She remained in Russia for a few years, but after a short period in prison in 1908 because of her brochure "Finland and Socialism," she lived in exile until the outbreak of the revolution in 1917. For almost a decade she led a peripatetic existence, living in Scandinavia, Germany, France, and Great Britain. At the command of the Russian Communist Party, she went to Sweden in 1914, but was deported due to an anti-militaristic article she wrote that antagonized Swedish authorities. She settled in Norway in 1915, but her stay there was interrupted by several lecturing tours to the United States during the course of the next two years. When the revolution in Russia was a reality, she immediately returned there and rose to prominence in Lenin's government. She became the first woman member of the Soviet Presidium and of the Bolshevik Party's Central Committee. She was also appointed Minister of Social Affairs, a position that offered her unique opportunities with regard to improving the position of women in the country.

During her exile from Russia, Kollontay belonged to the political circle around Karl Liebknecht and Rosa Luxemburg. She had no patience with Edward Bernstein's revisionism or the Fabians' incremental and slow advance toward socialism. She cooperated with Leon Trotsky for a short while working on the European edition of *Pravda*, but as the split between Lenin and Trotsky widened, she decided eventually to side with Lenin. On his part, Lenin had great respect for Kollontay, and at the meeting of a large socialist conference in Basel, Switzerland in 1912, he proposed that she should deliver the major address of the Russian delegation, since "she knows how to persuade people."[10]

A reporter from the Danish newspaper *Politiken* was also impressed with Alexandra's oratory when she spoke at a women's congress in Copenhagen in 1910. After her "intoxicating eloquence," all the other speakers appeared pale and dull according to a journalist, who described her impressive appearance in a tight-fitting black dress and with "a face which the horrors of the revolution had chiselled into stony hard and serious features. Only the eyes burned, and then the fire of revolutionary enthusiasm turned into flaming words," which Nobel Committee consultant, Jens Arup Seip, labels as "somewhat exaggerated."[11] Kollontay did not become a formal member of the Bolshevik Party until after the end of World War I. She must have had some reservations about the political course pursued by the party, as in 1921 she became one of the leaders of the so-called "workers' opposition." When the demands of this group were not met by the party leadership, she opted out of politics and became a diplomat. She headed the Soviet diplomatic office in Oslo, Norway, during two terms in the 1920s and was then posted in Stockholm from 1930 to 1945, the last few years as the ambassador. She was also a member of the Soviet Union's delegation to the League of Nations from 1935 until the outbreak of war in 1939. After the end of the war in 1945, she worked at the Department of Foreign Affairs in Moscow.

In his evaluation of her nomination for the Nobel Peace Prize in 1946, Jens Arup Seip states his impression that Kollontay was widely regarded as one of her nation's foremost citizens.[12]

Alexandra Kollontay was a prolific writer, and her productions include fiction, besides her numerous political essays and books. In Seip's opinion, her fictional works did not represent great art, but had intensity. The theoretical and historical works were first and foremost agitation concerning the position of women in society and the labor movement's role in furthering women's interests.[13]

Kollontay was an early convert to feminism. She was behind the establishment of the first socialist women's clubs in St. Petersburg already in 1907 and was a leading figure at international women's conferences. The titles of her essays and articles from this period reflect her preoccupation with women's issues: "In defense of motherhood" (1913), "Motherhood and society" (1916), and "The family and the communist society" (1918).

Like so many socialist feminists, Kollontay was very

critical toward any form of feminism not grounded in socialist principles. "Bourgeois feminism" was, in her opinion, extremely naïve with regard to its view of women's fight for justice. Neither culture nor information would liberate women; a complete revamping of the economic system was needed. Women's liberation, class struggle, and socialism were inextricably intertwined.

Similarly, Kollontay insisted that socialism was the necessary condition for peace. Only in a socialist society where the very causes of war, poverty, and class inequality had been eliminated, would war be impossible.

During World War I, when Kollontay lived in Norway after her expulsion from Sweden, she had close connections with Norwegian socialists, especially the leader of the Labor Party's women's movement, Martha Tynæs. Together, the two women worked to establish March 8 as an International Women's Day. In 1915, Kollontay also attended the national congress of the Labor Party, where the delegates voted to include a clause in the party program demanding demilitarization. Kollontay conveyed her enthusiasm for this decision to Lenin, but met a cold shoulder. Lenin considered the Norwegian position as an example of "petit bourgeois escapism from reality" and insisted that the demand for armed revolution as formulated in the Bolshevik party program be adhered to. "I consider it to be theoretically false and practically dangerous not to distinguish between the different types of war" was his position.[14]

Alexandra Kollontay remained loyal to the Soviet regime all her life, even though its policies were at odds with her own views regarding women's rights and sexual liberation as well as individual liberty. Her lifelong friend, Shlyapnikov-Belerin, with whom she shared a small cottage in the hills above Oslo during the First World War was, like so many revolutionary pioneers, excluded from the party as a dissident and died in one of Stalin's concentration camps. He had been Lenin's close friend and a member of his first government.

When the Second World War broke out in 1939, Kollontay was, along with Stalin, the only surviving member of the Soviet Union's first central committee.[15]

More than anything else, it was Kollontay's unstinting efforts to bring the Finnish-Soviet conflict (1939–1940) to an end that made her a Peace Prize candidate. She was most likely the one member of the Bolshevik party who possessed extensive knowledge of Finland, its people and political circumstances. Her cooperation with Finnish workers went back to the time before the twentieth century and continued through the years of her exile. She later commented about this period that in the conflict between the tsarist autocracy and the Finnish people, both her reason and her heart were on the side of the Finns.[16]

During the Second World War while Kollontay headed the Soviet diplomatic offices in Sweden, she was able to further Finland's interests by approaching the Kremlin, and she was also known to have made personal requests to Stalin on behalf of Finland. Even though she was no longer part of the Soviet ruling elite, as one of the few survivors of the "old guard," she still had access to the Kremlin and the possibility of exercising influence on its leaders.

Alexandra Kollontay was also nominated for the Nobel Peace Prize in 1947, but this time without appearing on the Nobel Committee's shortlist.

ELEANOR ROOSEVELT (1884–1962)

Fifteen people were nominated for the Nobel Peace Prize in 1947, two of them women. Six Norwegian parliamentarians were behind the proposal that Eleanor Roosevelt and Alexandra Kollontay should share the prize. As we know, none of them became prize winners, but Eleanor achieved a place on the Committee's shortlist and was evaluated as a candidate.

Eleanor Roosevelt grew up in New York. Her father, Elliot Roosevelt, was a very wealthy man, and the family's status was further enhanced when his brother, Theodore Roosevelt, became president of the United States in 1901. However, Eleanor did not experience a happy childhood. She was a clumsy, awkward, and serious kid and felt spurned by her mother. When their mother died at only 29 years of age, Eleanor and her two younger brothers went to live with their grandmother. The father, whom Eleanor adored, was banned from the home because of his alcoholism and dissolute lifestyle. He died before Eleanor was ten.

The happiest years of Eleanor's youth were spent at a British public school, where one of the teachers, Marie Souvestre, had a significant influence on her development. Back in the United States, she had her social debut at eighteen. This was expected of a young lady from "high society." Two years later she married her distant cousin, Franklin Delano Roosevelt, and over the next eleven years gave birth to five sons and one daughter. Homemaking and motherhood appeared to be her destiny.

However, the presidential election in 1912 resulted in quite a different course for the young homemaker. Franklin Delano Roosevelt was a lawyer, but his inclination was more in the direction of politics. He had supported the Democratic winner, Woodrow Wilson, who then tapped the young lawyer to be Assistant Secretary of the Navy in the new government. As the wife of a member of the cabinet, it was expected that Eleanor would participate in some form of volunteer activity. She chose to join the Red Cross, and it soon became evident that she possessed genuine administrative talents.

After the Democrats lost the 1920 election, the Roosevelt family returned to New York, where Franklin resumed his law practice, and Eleanor began to stake out her own career. The children were growing up, marriage had lost its bloom, and she longed to find engaging challenges. An ardent feminist, she chose to become a member of the League of Women Voters. One of her tasks was to write summaries of legislative proposals and political decisions that affected women, something that soon gave her sound insight into American politics. She also became active in the women's organization of the Democratic Party and rapidly acquired a position as a very popular writer and radio personality with a passion for social justice, women's rights, and the cause of peace. Without a doubt, her lifelong activity in these areas made her the most influential woman politician of this period in American history, even though she never held elective office.

American women had received the right to vote in national elections in 1920, but even so, relatively few became politically active. Eleanor Roosevelt was ahead of her time when she started creating influential women's networks long before the term was invented. She experienced ridicule and suspicion, but continued her efforts until she no longer could be overlooked. In solidarity with poor and unemployed women, she worked for laws that would secure employment at decent wages and shorter working hours. She fought for universal health insurance, against the opposition from the American Medical Association and the insurance industry, who were adamantly opposed to "socialized medicine."

As isolationist forces gained headway in the United States after the First World War, Eleanor Roosevelt was one of those who consistently worked for American entry into the League of Nations and ratification of the treaty to join the International Court of Justice. Together with Jane Addams, Emily Greene Balch, and Carrie Chapman Catt, she was among the country's most prominent internationalists at a time when the United States turned more and more isolationist, with anticommunist hysteria spreading and civil rights being set aside. The eager young director of the Bureau of Investigation (later named the Federal Bureau of Investigation, FBI), J. Edgar Hoover, began assembling his files on Eleanor Roosevelt and other active up-per-class women in the democratic camp.

Eleanor Roosevelt was decidedly not riding on her husband's coattails. In her comprehensive biography of Roosevelt, histo-rian Blanche Wiesen Cook argues persuasively that throughout the 1920s, it was actually Eleanor who was the family's most politically active member. She was also far more radical than her husband and less willing to let pragmatic politics and "re-alism" influence important policy choices and strategies. Thus, Eleanor was shocked when, during the electoral campaign of 1932, Franklin promised to work against American support for the League of Nations and the International Court of Justice, thereby securing the necessary votes from Texas and California for his candidacy at the Democrats' nominating convention. For Eleanor, who had worked so hard to change American policy in regard to the League of Nations and the International Court of Justice, and who knew that at heart, her husband real-ly shared her convictions, this was downright deceit.

Roosevelt's election as governor of New York in 1928 meant the beginning of an extremely busy period for Eleanor. In addition to her duties as First Lady of the state, with the travelling and entertaining it involved, she also founded and ran a school for girls, Todhunter School. Here she worked as a teacher and even wrote textbooks for use at the school. The first of these books, *When You Grow Up to Vote,* was a short intro-duction to the American political system, written in a way that would appeal to youngsters and get them interested in politics. Eleanor remained a member of the board of Todhunter School until 1938.

During the twelve years of Franklin Delano Roosevelt's presidency, Eleanor was her husband's active collaborator, functioning as advisor, critic, and often as his stand-in at po-litical engagements. Never before had the United States had a First Lady of her stature. The president's wife would appear, often incognito, at prisons, in ghettos of the big cities, in health-threatening factories, and in the poverty stricken rural areas of the deep South, where the economic conditions were often worse than anywhere else in the country. It seemed that wherever injustice existed, she would turn up to help. Through numerous articles and radio speeches, she conveyed her opinions regarding necessary changes, and she did not refrain from speaking out against her husband's policies if there were things she disapproved of.

Social justice, women's rights, and work for peace had been Eleanor Roosevelt's main concerns throughout the 1920s, and as First Lady she was determined to use her influence to further these causes. She was incensed when she realized that Roosevelt's New Deal was not intended to aid women. On the contrary, thousands of women were fired by the federal government after antinepotism rules were adopted. Women married to state employees must leave their jobs. Eleanor insisted that "a new deal" must also mean "a square deal" for women. She submitted long lists of competent women for consideration as appointees to federal offices. A direct result of this lobbying was that the first woman cabinet member in the United States, Frances Perkins, was appointed as Secretary of Labor by Roosevelt.

Thousands upon thousands of single, unemployed, and homeless women, maybe the most vulnerable victims of the Depression, weighed heavily on Eleanor's conscience. Together with her friends in the various women's networks, she helped initiate projects to secure housing, work, and decent wages for many of these unfortunate people. In her endeavors to win support for her projects, she used the press in a most professional way and established particularly good relationships with women journalists that were strengthened through weekly press conferences exclusively for female journalists.

While young, Eleanor Roosevelt had not been overly

concerned about the African-Americans' fight for civil rights. However, over time she became a strong opponent of all forms of racism. When Marion Anderson was prevented from singing in the concert hall of the Daughters of the American Revolution, Eleanor Roosevelt decided to sponsor an open air concert at the Lincoln Memorial in Washington, D.C., that attracted enormous crowds. She also reacted strongly against segregated seating at engagements where she was present and would sit down among the black people. If asked to move, she demanded a chair be placed in the middle of the aisle, between the "black" and the "white" sides of the room.[17]

Naturally, Eleanor Roosevelt encountered much opposition to her demonstrations in support of the rights of black people. It was regarded as very inappropriate when she brought her staff from the governor's mansion in New York along to the White House, thus integrating white and black employees at the very highest levels. Nor was it unproblematic to invite black friends as guests to the White House. When one of her good friends, the black civil rights activist Mary Bethune visited, Eleanor often went to the gate to meet her and walk up the stairs to the presidential residence in order to prevent unpleasant behavior from any of the guards.[18]

During the 1930s, America's black citizens were not only poor and discriminated against. Racial hatred also led to horrendous criminal acts, such as the many lynchings occurring in the South. Eleanor Roosevelt was very active in the movement to adopt a federal law against lynching, a law that guaranteed federal sanctions against the authorities in the states where such crimes were committed. The initiatives were resisted, in particular by southern politicians, who argued that such legislation would represent unacceptable interference in the constitutional rights of the states. To her chagrin, Eleanor did not even get the support of her husband, who was concerned about voter support in the South. Laws against lynching were not passed until many years later.

President Roosevelt was also unwilling to include support for international institutions such as the League of Nations and the International Court of Justice in his agenda. Eleanor, on her part, used her position as First Lady to support American participation in international work for peace. "War is old-fashioned," she declared in a speech she gave in 1935 in connection with the celebration of Carrie Chapman Catt's seventy-fifth birthday, underlining that war made everyone a loser, for "economic waste in one part of the world will have an economic effect in other parts of the world....as the rest of the world suffers, so eventually do we."[19] Naturally, this kind of talk was not popular in an America marked by communist hysteria. The president's wife was regarded by many as a dangerous socialist, an opponent of "law and order," and a threat to the "American way of life."

Among Eleanor Roosevelt's many books, several were written for children. *A Trip to Washington with Bobby and Betty* was characteristic of her desire to inform and educate children for their future civic roles. It was essential in a democratic society that youngsters be given solid information about the governmental system of their country.

The same desire to educate readers for democratic participation permeates the books designed for adult readers. In *This Troubled World* (1938), she addresses the problem of preventing international conflicts from developing into war. Even though critical of the way the League of Nations had functioned, Eleanor was convinced of the need for international forums as institutions for conflict solving, and she regretted that the work to convince the Senate to ratify U.S. membership in the International Court of Justice had failed.

Her message in *The Moral Basis of Democracy* (1940) is that active citizen involvement is the premise of a functioning democracy. Participatory democracy is the very foundation of democracy. The Nobel Peace Prize Committee's consultant sums up her attitude as follows: "One gets no living or sustainable democracy if the masses do not take an interest in politics, but are content to leave governing into the hands of a small group."[20]

Eleanor Roosevelt had high hopes that women would constitute the deciding factor in the elections of the future. She believed firmly that for democracy to function well, women must be active participants in the political system. As a coworker in *Democratic Digest,* the organ of the Democratic Party's women's movement, and a cofounder of "National Institute of Government" in 1940, she helped arrange a huge conference where several thousand American women gathered to examine political party programs concerning women's rights in a variety of areas.

After the end of the Second World War, Eleanor was appointed as a member of the U.S. delegation to the United Nations' General Assembly, and in 1946 she became leader of the UN Commission of Human Rights, whose foremost task was to prepare an international treaty protecting universal human rights. The Commission was charged with protecting the rights of minority groups and hindering discrimination on the basis of race, sex, religion, language, or ethnicity. In 1947 an editorial committee was appointed to make a draft proposal of the UN Declaration of Human Rights, and Eleanor became its leader.

Eleanor Roosevelt was nominated for the Nobel Peace Prize four times, in 1947, 1949, 1955, and 1959 and placed on the Committee's shortlist every year except 1955. The consultant who evaluated her candidacy in 1947, O. T. Røed, had very positive comments, pointing to the important challenge that lay ahead of her:

Eleanor Roosevelt is now in the midst of a great and

significant task. If she succeeds in accomplishing an international agreement where human rights are effectively ensured, she will forever have earned the admiration and gratitude of mankind.[21]

As we know, Eleanor Roosevelt succeeded. The United Nations' Declaration of Human Rights was adopted in 1948. However, her name was not on the list of candidates that year. The following year her name again appeared on the shortlist of candidates. Six members of the Norwegian Parliament submitted a strong proposal for her nomination. Great Britain's Lord Cecil nominated Roosevelt and the Commission secretary, René Cassin, as joint recipients.

A new consultant, Jens Arup Seip, had replaced O.T. Røed, and he did not share Røed's admiration for Roosevelt. On the basis of his perusal of the Commission's meeting protocols, he concluded that its success must be attributed to Cassin:

> Cassin was the leading member of the editorial committee, and the Commission did not appear to see itself as able to function without him. If Mrs. Roosevelt were to get the peace prize because of her work for the Declaration on Human Rights, it would be unreasonable if the prize were not also given to Cassin.[22]

However, meeting protocols are seldom infallible indicators of group influence and power. An able leader's role is to act as a referee, not to dominate the discussions. She must see to it that all the participants enjoy the opportunity of getting their points across. Indirectly, Jens Arup Seip admits as much when he mentions that as leader of the deliberations, Roosevelt could not participate in the debates of the Commission to the same degree as others.

In the final draft submitted for ratification by the Commission, the influence exercised by Roosevelt was apparent. According to Jens Arup Seip, there had been serious disagreements among the members regarding the text of the Declaration of Human Rights. Roosevelt, supported by Great Britain among others, underscored the importance of traditional, individual rights, while the Soviet Union's Pavlov emphasized economic and social rights. Eleanor Roosevelt, aware of the animosity in the American Congress against international bodies attempting to issue legally binding demands on the country, strongly insisted that the document must not be a legal text: "The declaration should not be in any sense a legislative document," she said during a Commission meeting on May 26, 1948.[23] Her view prevailed.

In 1959, just three years before her death, Eleanor Roosevelt was again nominated for the Peace Prize. This time, as well, her name was placed on the shortlist. But the evaluation by the young consultant, Kåre D. Tønnesson, made it quite clear that he was negative to the prospect of this "restlessly active woman" as he put it, ending up as a Nobel laureate. In his concluding remarks, he presents his view of Roosevelt in the following fashion:

> Probably the first to hit the eye is her naive attitude to the issues she is dealing with. She hardly delves deeply into the problems, and she feels no great need for precision or completeness in the way she presents them. Embarrassingly often, the reader encounters pure banalities or rather meaningless statements.[24]

In a little more congenial tone he concedes, however: "With all her impetuosity, she also appears to possess a certain humble attitude as a human being and as an American."[25]

This condescending view of Eleanor Roosevelt was certainly not shared by Aase Lionæs, longtime member of the Norwegian Nobel Committee and later its leader. She was an ardent admirer of Roosevelt and had worked for her candidature. Shortly before leaving the Committee in 1979, she was looking at all the portraits of the Peace Prize recipients in the Committee meeting room and remarked quietly: "As an old feminist I must say that there are two women I miss here, namely Eleanor Roosevelt and Alexandra Kollontay."[26]

Irwin Abrams would also have liked to see the two women sharing the prize in 1947. Reflecting on whether this award might have produced a positive effect on the climate of the cold war, he said, "Such a joint award in those early days of the cold war could have been a significant demonstration of the possibilities of the superpowers reaching an understanding."[27]

According to Gunnar Jahn, the Norwegian Nobel Committee leader for a quarter of a century (1941–1966), Eleanor Roosevelt was never seriously considered as a prize winner. In spite of the active support from Aase Lionæs, he noted in his diary in the fall of 1949, Roosevelt was beaten even before the race began.[28]

No Peace Prize was awarded in 1948. This would have been the logical time to give the prize to Roosevelt in recognition of her successful effort in getting the U.N. Declaration of Human Rights passed. Eleanor Roosevelt did, indeed, deserve "mankind's admiration and gratitude" for her work, as O.T. Røed had uttered the previous year.

WOMEN'S INTERNATIONAL LEAGUE FOR PEACE AND FREEDOM

WILPF was nominated for the Nobel Peace Prize three times, in 1955, 1957, and 1958. The first proposal was made by Professor Philip E. Jacob from the University of Pennsylvania and was supported by Emily Greene Balch, the earlier leader of WILPF and Nobel Prize winner in 1946. The organization was also nominated in 2013, but its history after 1960 will not be dealt with here, since this study is limited to the earlier period.

WILPF is the oldest continuously existing women's peace

organization, and its hundredth anniversary was celebrated in 2015. Its main office is located in Geneva, Switzerland, but it also maintains an office in New York. The League cooperates closely with the United Nations and related organizations, such as UNESCO.

WILPF was a direct offspring of the International Suffrage Alliance (ISA), already a solidly established organization in Europe at the time of the outbreak of World War I. The American Woman's Peace Party was launched in Washington, D.C., in January 1915 at the initiative of two well-known feminists and peace activists, Jane Addams and Carrie Chapman Catt. About 3,000 American women joined them. The party adopted a radical program demanding voting rights for women and the immediate assembly of an international women's congress to protest against the war.

Plans for an International Women's Peace Conference, to be held in Berlin in June 1915, were already in the making before the outbreak of the war, but after the war was a reality, the German contingent of ISA cancelled the conference. Incensed women peace activists in Europe reacted with disbelief to this decision, and the leader of the suffrage movement in the Netherlands, Dr. Aletta Jacobs, supported by Hungarian feminists, hurriedly arranged a meeting in Amsterdam in February 1915 where German, British, and Belgian women could attend. They agreed to extend invitations to a women's congress to be held in The Hague the last three days of April 1915. Dr. Jacobs took on the responsibility for planning the event, and she immediately requested that Jane Addams accept the role as president of the congress. Addams, along with a strong American delegation, arrived just in time for the opening ceremony. Dr. Jacobs welcomed the 1,136 delegates and over 300 guests and observers from both neutral and warring nations and emphasized that the women had gathered in order to protest against war and frame resolutions to hinder future wars.[29] To secure continuity in the work until the war ended, the congress decided to establish The International Committee of Women for Permanent Peace, ICWPP. Jane Addams was elected to serve as its president and Rosika Schwimmer became vice president.

As soon as the war was over, ICWPP set the wheels in motion for another women's peace congress, which was held in Zürich, Switzerland, in 1919. The leaders had initially wanted to meet in Paris in order to be able to have direct impact on the Versailles peace talks, but decided instead to arrange their own, alternative congress when it became clear that their presence in Paris would not be welcome. The resolutions adopted by the women's congress were extremely critical of the terms imposed by the allied leaders on Germany and Austria because they were sure to spawn disorder and new wars. Plans for regular peace conferences in the years ahead were approved, and the congress also decided on a change of name: Women's International League for Peace and Freedom (WILPF), replacing the cumbersome ICWPP. The new name was a signal that the organization's purpose still remained to fight for women's freedom, voting rights, and a society with equality between the sexes.

After the Second World War, WILPF received permanent consulting status at the United Nations, ECOSOC, FAO, and UNESCO. The organization has consistently pursued a dual course: On the one side, influencing popular opinion, on the other exercising pressure on national and international institutions and decision makers. A substantial part of WILPF's work has been focused on the United Nations, both with regard to support for the organization in the various membership countries and concerning the policies it pursues.

WILPF is politically neutral but has been clearly influenced by the radical attitudes characterizing many women's organizations both during the inter-war period and the time after World War II. The program adopted in 1934 states the organization's main purpose to be working for the elimination of the various political, social, psychological, and economic reasons behind wars, thereby altering the social system in such a way that economic and political equality may be realized without regard to race, gender, or religion. The ultimate goal is to attain an economic system based on human needs, not on regard for profits.

After the Second World War, WILPF consistently underlined the importance of social and economic reforms as a basic condition for peace, while at the same time protesting against militarism and the armaments race. "Disarm the world to build the world" was the slogan adopted by the League's congress in 1953. Human rights, personal freedom, and equality have steadily received a more prominent place in League policy. Besides equal rights for men and women, protests against race discrimination and demands for elimination of capital punishment are examples of causes the organization has fronted in recent decades.

Historian Jens Arup Seip was the Nobel Committee's consultant when WILPF was first nominated for the peace prize in 1955. In his recommendation to the Committee, he notes that it is difficult to point to concrete results from WILPF's activity. Its role, he says, is to influence public opinion, to place new questions and problems on the political agenda, and to suggest creative solutions to these problems. To illustrate this, he cites what WILPF's secretary general, Gertrude Baer, wrote in 1951:

> WILPF has headed the charge as a pioneer. We did not wait until others assumed the mantle of leadership or accepted what we did. We knew what we desired in international work. We planned it carefully. We exerted leadership, even in cases where our actions were considered as quite impractical, fantastic, and utopian. Sometimes they were just that. A year or two later, often only a few months later, our actions turned out to have

been realistic, practical, and worthy of emulation.[30]

The international leader of WILPF at this time was Norway's Marie Lous Mohr, who served in that position between 1952 and 1956 after many years as a leader of the Norwegian branch of the organization as well as a member of WILPF's international board. She was highly respected, but her leadership coincided with a very difficult period for WILPF. The cold war dominated international relations, and since the Norwegian branch had assumed a strong stance against the country's NATO membership, rumors spread that WILPF was somehow tainted with communist sympathies. The leaders' attempts to calm people's fears did not stem the unrest, and WILPF faced a great many cancelled memberships in Norway, which in turn led to many of the local branches closing down. The cold war climate was therefore far from favorable to WILPF when it was nominated for the Nobel Peace Prize.

Although WILPF, probably more than many other candidates for the Nobel Peace Prize, met the criteria stipulated by Alfred Nobel in his will, namely, that the prize recipient should have worked for international understanding and for demilitarization and peace conferences, the organization was passed over by the Nobel Committee. No Peace Prize was awarded either in 1955 or in 1956, as none of the candidates appeared sufficiently qualified.

GERTRUDE BAER (1889–1959)

When WILPF was proposed as a candidate for the Nobel Peace Prize in 1955, the organization's secretary general, Gertrude Baer, was also nominated. Both Baer and WILPF were placed on the Committee's shortlist. Baer was then nominated every year for the remainder of the decade, altogether five times. In 1957 she was once more placed on the Committee's shortlist.

Gertrude Baer was German and grew up in Hamburg. After language studies in Hamburg, Leipzig, and Munich, she was hired in 1919 to work at the office for women's rights in the government's Department of Social Affairs. Even though she was not a member of any political party, her sympathies were clearly on the left side of the political spectrum. Like so many other women Nobel Peace Prize candidates, Baer had been recruited early into the feminist movement and was active in the fight for women's voting rights. For many years she was also a regular contributor to the magazine *Die Frau im Staat.*

World War I made Gertrude Baer join the peace movement. She did not take part in the great women's conference in The Hague in 1915, but when WILPF opened its congress in Zürich in 1919, she was a member of the German delegation, and, as a representative of German youth, she delivered a passionate speech that brought her great applause and a lot of attention. "From this moment an essential part of her activity, and soon all of her activity, was tied to the Women's International League for Peace and Freedom," writes Jens Arup Seip in his comments to the Norwegian Nobel Committee.[31] She was, says Seip, quite obviously the driving force of WILPF's German section, where she was a member of the board from 1921 until she had to flee to Switzerland when Hitler came to power in 1933. She had worked tirelessly against German militarization, but also engaged herself in social questions like women's equality, the rights of children born outside of wedlock, and the fight for abortion. "Here is a mixture of peace politics, social politics, and women's rights, with an emphasis on the first," writes Seip.[32]

In 1929, when WILPF adopted a leadership model with three equal members on its presidium, Gertrude Baer became a member of the troika, and from June 1940, she worked at the League's office in New York. According to Marie Lous Mohr, the leader of the Norwegian section of WILPF, it was greatly due to Baer's immense efforts that WILPF remained organizationally intact during the war.[33] However, the war caused tremendous damage. In countries ruled by the Nazis, WILPF's offices were often in ruins, and many of its members had died in concentration camps after their arrests for underground activities.

In addition to responsibility for rebuilding the organization in Europe, Baer now also assumed the challenging task of establishing WILPF in countries where it had not yet achieved any following. She believed that WILPF must become an important force in underdeveloped areas, a loud voice against racism and for social justice, freedom, and national independence.

Gertrude Baer left WILPFs executive board in 1946 in order to be the League's representative at the United Nations, but in 1950 she was back as leader of the main office in Geneva, with responsibility for publication of the magazine *Peace and Freedom*. In 1952, she was appointed secretary general of the organization, and more than anyone else she was now responsible for shaping the League's political profile through reports and articles.

"She represents the identity of the Women's League," wrote Jens Arup Seip in his evaluation of her candidacy. Still, he was not willing to give her a clear and positive endorsement in his summary to the Nobel Committee. "She has something stern, intense, and uncompromising about her," he wrote, and characterized her as an action-oriented person with an iron will. "One imagines that she is more respected than loved by her fellow workers. She appears to lack Balch's lighter side and deep human empathy, and has probably no place for humor, but she is undoubtedly a significant person," is his final comment.[34] It is hard to imagine a man with an admitted iron will and action orientation getting such qualities noted as negative. Did conventional gender expectations have something to do with the consultant's remarks?

KATHARINE BRUCE GLASIER (1868–1950)

Among the twenty-one candidates nominated for the Nobel Peace Prize in 1948, there were only two women: the veteran Rosika Schwimmer and the English philanthropist, feminist, and socialist Katharine Bruce Glasier, a leading personality in the early labor movement in Great Britain. She was nominated by Gilbert McAllister, member of the British House of Commons, for having "devoted an entire lifetime to the cause of peace and international friendship."[35] Katharine Bruce Glasier grew up in a liberal home. Her father, Samuel Conway, was a clergyman, and both he and his wife, Amy Curling, were tolerant and broadminded people who regarded it as self-evident that their daughter should receive as good an education as their sons did. At a time when very few women had a chance to get higher education, Katharine completed studies at Cambridge University and then taught at a girls' high school for some time.

Early on, Katharine Conway declared herself a feminist and socialist. She became a member of the Fabian Society and befriended people like George Bernard Shaw as well as Sidney and Beatrice Webb. Before long she entered the lecture circuit on behalf of the Fabian Society and became a popular speaker, talking about subjects like suffrage for women and other social and political issues.

In 1893, Katharine joined the Independent Labour Party (ILP). This party had a clear Christian and socialist profile that corresponded well with her own faith. The same year she married the poet John Bruce Glasier who was also a political activist on the left and a future leader of ILP. Over the next few decades, Katharine Bruce Glasier became one of Great Britain's most influential women. She was in constant demand as a public speaker and also became known as an author and journalist. From 1916 on, she served for many years as editor of *The Labour Leader* and earned a reputation as an avid opponent of war and militarism. She was one of the founders of Save the Children, the institution that contributed to saving the lives and welfare of so many youngsters during World War I. As a Quaker, she also participated actively in the international aid programs of the Society of Friends.

After almost forty years as a member of ILP, Katharine Bruce Glasier refused to go along with the party when it decided to cut its ties to the Labor Party in 1932. She decided to remain a member of the mother party and was exuberant when Labor won the election in 1945 and formed its first majority government. Until her death she continued as an active spokesperson for ILP and celebrated her 80th birthday lecturing for an audience of more than 1,000 persons on "The Religion of Socialism" shortly before being nominated as a candidate for the Nobel Peace Prize.

MARIA MONTESSORI (1870–1952)

The Italian physician, Maria Montessori, became internationally famous early in the twentieth century as the founder of a new and groundbreaking pedagogical method, the Montessori Method. She was nominated as a candidate for the Nobel Peace Prize three times, in 1949, 1950, and 1951. In 1950, she was the only female candidate among a total of twenty-eight nominees. She never attained a place on the Nobel Committee's shortlist.

Maria was the first Italian woman to obtain a medical degree when she passed her exams at the University of Rome with excellent results in 1896. But it was as a school reformer that she would become internationally famous. Nothing in her background indicated that she was destined to exert a revolutionary influence on child rearing and children's schooling. Her father, Allesandro Montessori, had been a member of the Italian military and ended up in the country's bureaucracy. He was "an old-fashioned gentleman of conservative temper and military habits" writes Montessori's biographer, Rita Kramer.[36] He was, not surprisingly, irritated by his daughter's choice of profession, considering it inappropriate for a woman to become a physician. However, Maria's mother, Renilde Stoppani, was of another opinion and supported her daughter in her quest for a university degree in medicine. Maria had early showed herself to be an enterprising child, with definite abilities as a leader. The odds that she would get accepted as a medical student seemed unlikely at first, but she was admitted, the only woman in the class.

After finishing her degree, Montessori accepted a position at a psychiatric clinic in Rome, and here she developed an even stronger interest in children's development. She pursued pedagogical studies at the university in Rome and gradually developed her famous method with regard to the education of small children, based on solid medical, psychiatric, and pedagogical knowledge. What is characteristic of Montessori's method, according to the Norwegian pedagog, Dr. Eva Nordland, is that it "builds on the child's natural quest for development and activity."[37] Instead of the child adapting to the school and the demands of the teachers, the school must "follow the child" and be child-centred.

Maria got an excellent opportunity to test her theories when she was asked to become leader of a school for "problem children," children with learning disabilities, behavioral problems, or different forms of functional handicaps. The school opened in 1906 and was named Casa dei Bambini (Children's House). The physical environment in the school was adjusted to suit every child, with light chairs and tables that were easily moved and were the right size for little people. The children's intellectual curiosity and orientation toward activity were stimulated, and they were allowed to play, experiment, and enjoy the delight of mastering practical tasks. The results were astounding, and soon the word spread in both Europe and other parts of the world about Maria Montessori and her school. Gradually, this led to requests for her help in training teachers to use the "Montessori method." Before long, Montessori's methods became widespread both in the West and in parts of Asia, and they contributed to radical change in the attitudes toward child rearing and educational policies.

Maria Montessori's antifascist attitudes created problems for her in Benito Mussolini's dictatorial Italy, and by 1939, she was happy to accept the invitation from Indian theosophists to give a series of lectures in their country. The onset of the war made her stay there longer than planned, and she remained in India until 1947. During these years, "education for peace" became of great concern to her, and she attempted to fuse her own theories of education to Mahatma Gandhi's philosophy of nonviolence. However, as Montessori had never been directly involved in any kind of traditional peace work, the Norwegian Nobel Committee apparently did not evaluate her work to be of sufficient relevance to commend her as a Peace Prize recipient. The "broader peace concept" which the Committee embraced a few years later, would perhaps have made Montessori appear as a suitable candidate for the Prize. However, some time had yet to pass before the Committee was ready to accept the idea that activities unrelated to traditional peace activism might, in fact, contribute to hinder war and further peace.

EVA PERON (1919–1952)

The same year that Maria Montessori was nominated for the first time, 1949, the Nobel Committee received a proposal suggesting that the dictator of Argentina, Juan Peron, ought to share the Peace Prize with his wife, Eva Peron.

Eva Duarte Peron grew up in poverty in a small rural village in Argentina, where her mother ran a boarding house. Eva was next to the youngest of five children. When only 16 years old, she moved to Buenos Aires, hoping for an acting career. By the time she was 25, she had established a name for herself both on stage and in film and was attached to one of the big radio stations in the country. In 1944, she met Juan Peron, a military officer and widower, twenty-four years her senior. They married the next year, and in 1946, she played an active role in the political campaign that led him to power as Argentina's president. It was the first time that a woman had played the role of a political actor in Argentina, but the beautiful and charismatic Eva soon became a favorite of the people and far more popular than her husband.

Eva Peron never held any official political position, but with her genuine concern for the poor and the ostracized, she quickly became the strongest voice in the government's sociopolitical efforts. She appealed to the underprivileged and used her influence both to get people appointed and fired as members of the cabinet or as leaders in the mighty labor unions. She supported the demands of the workers, helped them get generous wage increases, and served as a de facto minister of labor. Welfare for women, children, and older persons was high on her agenda, and projects were launched to build schools, nursing homes, and orphanages. The First Lady received visits every day from poor people, listened to their complaints, and contributed to increasing support for Peron's regime among the masses of less fortunate citizens.

Women's suffrage was one of the causes Eva Peron was deeply committed to, and in 1949, she spearheaded the founding of the first great women's party in Argentina, the Peronista Feminist Party.[38] Argentina's first elected female president, Christina Fernandez, has acknowledged that both she and her generation of the country's women as a whole owe a huge debt of gratitude to Eva Peron for her contribution to secure gender equality in Argentina. However, neither Eva nor Juan Peron was ever engaged in direct work for the cause of peace, and the Nobel Committee did not place either of them on its shortlist after having received their nomination in 1949.

PRINCESS WILHELMINA (1880–1962)

When the School of Law at the University of Leyden in the Netherlands nominated their candidate for the Nobel Peace Prize in 1951, it also requested that the name of the nominee be kept secret and that the name must not be publicized later if the candidate did not receive the award. The person in question was Her Royal Highness Princess Wilhelmina, earlier Queen Wilhelmina of the Netherlands for half a century, from 1898 until she abdicated in 1948.

In their proposal, the law professors pointed to Wilhelmina's work for peace during many decades and her efforts both in 1899 and 1907 to persuade world political leaders to support the peace conferences promoted by Russia's Tsar Nicholas II.

After the outbreak of World War II in 1939, she, along with the King of Belgium, contacted all the warring parties and offered her services as a mediator in order to obtain an end to the conflict. When Hitler's forces invaded the Netherlands, Queen Wilhelmina left her country and lived in exile, playing an active role in the attempts to organize a new world order that would help avoid war in the future.

"We recall especially the far-seeing radio speech of 7th December, 1942, which at that time made such a strong impression throughout the world" wrote the nominators in their letter to the Nobel Committee, and they also referred to the fact that after her abdication, Princess Wilhelmina had conducted important work furthering peace through her support for the ecumenical movement.[39]

ELISABETH ROTTEN (1882–1964)

In 1952, only two women were nominated for the Nobel Prize, namely Dr. Elisabeth Rotten and Barbara Waylen. Dr. Rotten was proposed by British Quakers for her work with prisoners of war during and after World War I and her extensive work for peace during the interwar period. She was the founder of Children's International Village (Pestalozzi) in Switzerland and had significant influence on the development of pedagogical thinking in Europe.

Elisabeth Friederike Rotten was born in Berlin, where her Swiss parents resided. After graduating from high school, she studied languages and literature in Berlin and Marburg. Later, she obtained a doctoral degree and was acclaimed as an expert on Goethe. In the fall of 1913, she was appointed to a position at Cambridge University, where she taught literature and languages.

World War I caused her career to take another course than it probably would have if the war had not broken out. As a Swiss citizen, Rotten was able to construct an impressive aid program for German, Austrian, and Hungarian prisoners of war. Through her contact with the Society of Friends, the Quakers, she was an active partner in the organization of relief programs benefiting millions of starving German children. She became a convinced pacifist, and in the spring of 1915, she was a delegate to the women's congress in The Hague. In 1919, she gave a lecture at WILPF's congress in Zürich.

After the end of the First World War, Elisabeth Rotten lived in Germany until 1934, when she moved to her parents' homeland, Switzerland, because of the Nazi takeover in Germany. She was active in the peace movement and translated Philip Noel-Baker's book, *The Arms Race: A Programme for World Disarmament,* into German. She also wrote a biography of Noel-Baker, who received the Nobel Peace Prize in 1959.

Working with the Pestalozzi children's villages, which she had helped organize, took up a great deal of her time in the years before her death.

BARBARA WAYLEN (1906–1980)

The second woman nominated in 1952 for the Nobel Peace Prize was Barbara Waylen from Oxford, England. She was nominated by Professor Norman Bentwich on behalf of the "Friends of the Hebrew University of Jerusalem."

In his nomination of Waylen, professor Bentwich drew attention to a book she had edited, published in 1951, *Creators of the Modern Spirit,* with the subtitle, *Towards a Philosophy of Faith.* According to Bentwich, the main purpose of the book was to spread understanding and goodwill among all peoples and races. The book contained articles by prominent people, among them Mahatma Gandhi. The authors related their search for a deeper meaning in life and the need for peace and understanding among the world's nations.

A copy of this book reached the Dutch queen, Juliana, who was impressed and decided, together with several friends, to invite Barbara Waylen to a series of peace conferences to be held at the Oude Loo castle near Apeldoorn in the Netherlands. The first of these conferences took place in July 1951, but Waylen was unable to attend. She did, however, send supporting greetings to the participants, calling for the establishment of a universal church in which all men of good will, all religions and nations could cooperate in the work to attain international peace.

Four months later, the second conference took place. Barbara Waylen and Eleanor Roosevelt were among those invited to stay as special guests at the Oude Loo castle, the residence of Princess Wilhelmina, the former queen. Here the organizers, speakers, and guests mingled, discussed, ate and slept during the three days of the conference. Waylen expressed hopes that Queen Juliana would assume leadership of a movement toward world government, as a "Queen of Peace."

A third conference was held in the summer of 1952, but by this time serious discord had erupted within the group leadership. One of its most prominent leaders, Wim Kaiser, was strongly influenced by a faith healer named Greet Hofmans, who claimed to possess spiritual powers that enabled her to communicate directly with God and receive commands from the Lord. Kaiser insisted on submission to Hofmans' ideas and had little sympathy for Waylen's dreams of a universal church where people of all creeds could meet and work harmoniously towards world government. At the November 1951 conference there were already signs of protest against Wim Kaiser's increasingly authoritarian leadership. Both Waylen and Roosevelt had reacted against his lack of humility and respect for the opinions of others. Roosevelt, in particular, had exchanged sharp words with Kaiser, expressing her dislike of people who claimed to have a hotline to heaven and the Almighty. Not surprisingly, neither Waylen nor Eleanor Roosevelt were invited to the third peace conference.

Four years later, in 1956, a constitutional crisis developed in the Netherlands, which involved the Queen and her close friends in the group now known as the Oude Loo group. An anonymous writer published a report claiming that the marriage of Queen Juliana and the Prince Consort, Prince Bernhard, was breaking up, because of her close connections to what was described as a dangerous sect of extremist peace lovers (pacifists) who posed serious threats to the state. Only several decades later were researchers able to unravel the facts behind this bizarre story. The source behind the rumors was Prince Bernhard himself, who succeeded in persuading the government that the Queen must give up her "dangerous friends," perform her constitutional duties as head of the nation, and let the prince perform his manly duty as head of the household! Juliana's friends were declared unwanted at the palace, and her dreams of working for international peace were thwarted. The royal marriage was saved when Juliana gave up her dear friendships and her religious mission. Barbara Waylen's contacts with the Dutch Royal Court came to a close, as well as her dream of seeing Juliana as "the Queen of Peace." Her letters to the queen between 1952 and 1956 were never answered.

Waylen continued her work for international arbitration and conciliation. Other books she authored include *The Story of Frances Banks: The Great Seeker* and *Evidence of Divine Purpose*. She died at the age of 74 in 1980.[40]

MARGARET SANGER (1880–1966)

In 1952, the Norwegian Nobel Committee found yet another instance when the nomination of a famous American woman was on its table, namely Margaret Sanger. Margaret Louise Higgins Sanger grew up in a poor family with an Irish background. Her father was an ardent socialist, politically active on the left side of the political spectrum, and Margaret declared herself early on as both a feminist and a socialist. Her radicalism had, most likely, a great deal to do with her mother's fate: After eighteen pregnancies and eleven childbirths, she died, only 50 years of age. Poor people had no access to the "French products" that women from the higher social strata could get hold of.

Margaret studied to be a nurse, and together with her husband, architect William Sanger, she was attracted to the radical political environment in Greenwich Village, and soon became known as a pioneer in the fledgling movement for sex education and family planning in the United States. As a nurse in the slum districts of New York, she saw her mother's tragedy repeated over and over. The debasing conditions experienced by poverty-stricken women, worn out from frequent childbirths and ignorant about how to prevent unwanted pregnancies, infuriated her. New York laws forbid all information about "birth control," a concept launched by Sanger. She decided simply to ignore the law and resort to civil disobedience.

In her own magazine, *Woman Rebel*, she wrote a series of articles called "What Every Girl Should Know" about sexuality, pregnancy, and family planning. The publication was soon banned, and in 1914, she was charged with printing materials containing "obscene information." Sanger fled to Europe, thus avoiding arrest. While abroad, she studied policies regarding family planning in various countries, and back in the United States, together with her sister, Ethel Byrne, she started in 1916 the country's first birth control clinic, modelled on the clinics she had seen in Europe. On the clinic's opening day, there was a long waiting line outside of women who wanted information. Nine days later the authorities closed the clinic, and both Sanger and her sister were charged and convicted. However, the huge attention created around the whole affair also contributed to placing the issue on the public agenda, and the ensuing debate caused American public opinion to change and the laws to be amended.

The American Birth Control League, which later changed its name to the Planned Parenthood Federation of America, was founded in 1929. During the following years, Margaret Sanger spent a great deal of time on international travel, helping to build up birth control clinics both in Europe and Asia. Before the Second World War broke out in 1939, she had visited both China and Japan. In 1952, at a conference on family planning in Bombay, she was one of the founders of a new, international umbrella organization, the Planned Parenthood Federation. The next year she was elected president of this organization, a position she retained until 1959.

In her own country, Margaret Sanger did not experience

the final victory of the cause she had spent a lifetime fighting for. She died seven years before the 1973 U.S. Supreme Court Roe v. Wade decision that declared women had a constitutional right to terminate unwanted pregnancies.

Margaret Sanger was nominated as a candidate for the Nobel Peace Prize five times: Every year from 1953 till 1956 and then the last time in 1960. Twice, in 1953 and in 1960, the Committee placed her on its shortlist, the only woman so honored those years. In 1960, she was the candidate who received the most nominations—altogether twenty proposals listed her name. Certainly, there can be no doubt about her role in history. Maybe more than anyone else, she contributed to the liberation of women, regarded by many as the most important revolution of our time. Nobel laureate Pearl Buck, one of those proposing Sanger for the Peace Prize, stated that she had led the possibly greatest humanitarian fight of our era and was always faithful to her idea, "an idea she foresees will someday lead to world peace."[41] Knut Getz Wold, who wrote the evaluation of her as a candidate in 1953, also underlined the importance of her work for the cause of peace and noted her insistence that family planning must be seen in a wider, international context:

> The far too strong population increase in great parts of the world created poverty and unrest. The population pressure in the overpopulated and underdeveloped countries led to military expansion and was a danger to world peace.[42]

Getz Wold also pointed to the fact that it was precisely her achievement in these areas that were mentioned in the many proposals that were submitted. A decision to give her the Prize, he said, could be seen as "naturally related to the award given Lord Boyd Orr in 1949 because of the intimate connection between the question of nutrition and that of overpopulation."[43] It is interesting that Knut Getz Wold here clearly mentioned the so-called "enlarged concept of peace," which was implicit in the Boyd Orr award, although not clearly articulated by the Nobel Committee itself.

When Margaret Sanger was nominated in 1960, the consultant to the Nobel Committee, Preben Munthe, was far less positive in his comments than Knut Getz Wold had been. Ms. Sanger's contributions to the family planning conferences she had participated in were minimal, according to him, and mostly confined to short but enthusiastic greetings to the delegates. As far as questions related to demography and overpopulation, she had little to say but let the scientists dominate the debates.[44]

One could ask whether it would not have been more desirable to evaluate the total effect of Ms. Sanger's global work over a lifetime, rather than her lectures to international audiences in her old age.

The Nobel Committee postponed its decision in 1960, and the next year they awarded the reserved Prize to Albert John Lutuli from South Africa for his work against apartheid.[45]

HELEN KELLER (1880–1968)

The story of Helen Adams Keller, who was nominated for the Nobel Peace Prize in 1958, is well known across the world. She grew up in Alabama, where her father, Captain Arthur Keller, was a newspaper editor and a solid pillar of society. All seemed to point to a safe and happy childhood when little Helen, only one year old, got ill and became totally blind and deaf. Without any possibility of communicating with others, Helen developed into a furious little monster who tyrannized the whole family with her frequent outbursts of anger. A miraculous change occurred after Anne Sullivan was hired as a governess for Helen. She taught the little girl to speak and to read Braille and guided her through the regular school curricula. When she was twenty, Helen was admitted to one of the most prestigious schools in the United States, Radcliffe College, and graduated with honors four years later.

Early on, Helen Keller turned to writing as a career, published several books, and made a lifelong humanitarian contribution to aid not only the deaf and blind, but also others suffering from various kinds of functional disorders. "The effort to secure that all people with handicaps are accorded their self-evident human rights has been alpha and omega in all of Helen Keller's endeavors," wrote August Schou in his evaluation of Keller's candidacy for the Nobel Committee.[46] Like so many of the female Peace Prize candidates, Helen Keller had a radical bent, and she declared herself to be a dedicated socialist. In a conversation with Andrew Carnegie, she was reported to have blamed him for not sharing her socialist attitudes.[47] Socialism also colored her understanding of international conflicts: She regarded war as a result of the existing capitalistic system.

The leader of the Norwegian Liberal Party, Helge Seip, was among those proposing Helen Keller for the Nobel Peace Prize. In his nomination of her, he wrote that Keller had been a traveling ambassador throughout the world "for helpfulness, goodwill, and for deconstruction of barriers between people from different races and environments." A Peace Prize to Keller, he added, "will be a natural continuation of the course that led to Albert Schweitzer obtaining the Prize. It will be an appeal to all those forces in the world who struggle to see understanding and goodwill become a stronger power both within and between nations than is the case today."[48] Clearly implicit in this statement is Seip's belief that the Peace Prize awarded to Schweitzer represented a departure from an old tradition and the introduction of a new course that he clearly supported. The "enlarged concept of peace" had begun to characterize the nominations and awarding of the Peace Prizes: Efforts to create a good society represent work for peace. Hence, the Nobel Committee must not restrict its attention just to people who have engaged themselves in "traditional" peace activism, such as demilitarization, organization of peace congresses, and the pursuit of international brotherhood. It must be legitimate also to award the Prize to those who, in a wider sense, have contributed to the creation of a better society and thus to a re-duced basis for conflict. In this sense Helen Keller was, indeed, a worthy candidate for the Peace Prize.

LADY BADEN-POWELL (1889–1977)

Six Norwegian parliamentarians, representing different parties, stood behind the Nobel Peace Prize nomination in 1959 for the leader of the World Association of Girl Guides and Girl Scouts, Lady Baden-Powell from Great Britain. In their letter of nomination, the politicians underscored that Lady Baden-Powell had consistently emphasized the idea of "women's great importance regarding attitudes toward peace, attitudes that must be fostered among youth. She has spent all her energy attempting to realize this idea during her many trips all over the world."[49]

Lady Baden-Powell's maiden name was St. Clair Soames. Her first name was Olave, as she was reputedly named after Saint Olav, the Norwegian king who was sainted by the Catholic Church after his death in 1030. When she was only 19 years old, Olave accompanied her father, a wealthy brewery owner, on a trans-Atlantic trip to Jamaica. During the voyage, she met Robert Baden-Powell, thirty-two years her senior, and fell in love with him. Before the ship reached port, they were engaged, and a few months later they married.

Lord Baden-Powell had started the British scouting move-ment in 1903, and Olave now became a very active partner in the work of the organization. In 1916, she was elected leader of the Girl Guides in the British Empire, and two years later she began her work to gather all Girl Scouts in the world under a cross-national umbrella association. An international council was established in 1919, and thereafter international conferences met every other year. In 1930, this international council was replaced by the more formal World Association of Girl Guides and Girl Scouts, and at the world conference in London the same year, Lady Baden-Powell was appointed "Chief Guide of the World." Her home, Pax Hill in Hampshire, became from then on the headquarters for both the British and the international girl guide movement, and scouts from all corners of the world often visited there in order to meet Lady Baden-Powell and plan strategies for their work.

According to Kåre D. Tønnesson, who wrote the evaluation of Baden-Powell in 1959, the ideals of tolerance and work for peace constituted "ever present themes in her speeches to scouts and scouting leaders and in her conversations with them."[50] Concerning the direct influence of the scouting movement on the work for peace, however, he maintained that it is "hardly possible to point to concrete results of its work for the cause of peace." But then he continued:

> Anyway, it is still natural to think that the scouting movement, simply because it works with children and youth, is among those organizations which indirectly possess a relatively great possibility to influence also individuals who do not participate in it.[51]

"Indirect influence" on the work for peace was not sufficient to earn Baden-Powell a Prize in 1959. The Nobel Prize winner that year was Philip John Noel-Baker, who had spent a lifetime working directly for peace, demilitarization, and disarmament.

CHAPTER 4
CONCLUSIONS

What conclusions are suggested by the research presented in this study? First, the women themselves—the thirty-six women who, in spite of prejudices and patriarchal social norms, succeeded in attracting so much attention to their work that they were nominated as candidates for the Nobel Peace Prize. Who were they? What characteristics did they share with the male nominees, and how were they different from them? Were men prioritized by the Nobel Committee? Were the women victims of discrimination?

Just like the men, most of the women candidates for the Peace Prize came from upper-middle-class backgrounds. A few had ties to the aristocracy, and there were also some who grew up in poverty. As a whole, however, they were solidly planted in the comfortable higher echelons of society. Consequently, most of them were well educated even though during this period women generally had to be satisfied with only elementary school training or even less. The female Nobel Prize candidates were career women and organizationally active. They were teachers, lawyers, physicians, professors, and journalists, and many were able administrators of various reform movements.

They were also white. Not a single one of the thirty-six women nominated between 1901 and 1960 came from Africa or Asia. Geographically, almost all were from Europe or the United States. A couple of them came from South America, and one from the Soviet Union. In this, too, they resembled the men. The first nonwhite Nobel Peace Prize laureate was Ralph Bunche in 1950. Argentina's Carlos Saavedra Lamas was the first person outside Western Europe or the United States to be awarded the Prize. And, just like the men, most of the women were not exactly young when nominated. Eva Peron was, at 30, the very youngest woman ever nominated during this period.

Statistically speaking, it is not possible to accuse the Nobel Committee of direct gender discrimination: From 1901 to 1960, over 1,000 nominations arrived at the Nobel Institute in Oslo. Some of the proposed candidates were organizations, but the vast majority of them were men. During the entire period, only thirty-six women were nominated.

Considering the low number of women candidates for the Prize, the Nobel Committee may indeed be regarded as "women friendly" rather than the opposite, both with respect to Prize recipients and to women attaining a position on the shortlists. The root cause behind women's absence from the list of Nobel laureates was, of course, women's position in society and rigid sex role expectations. Relatively few women received an education or career experiences that qualified them for an active participation in society. This was reflected in the low number of female candidates for the Peace Prize during these first years. Usually, only one or two women were nominated, and some years none.

A Condescending View of Women?

Quite apart from dry statistics, it is possible to look at the question from another point of view. A survey of the candidate evaluations by the consultants to the Nobel Committee reflects in several instances a more or less subtle condescension toward women. First, one may mention the many nominations before Bertha von Suttner and Jane Addams finally won their Prizes—five in the case of von Suttner and eight for Addams. It also appears insulting that two of the three female laureates during these sixty years, Jane Addams and Emily Greene Balch, had to share the Prize with a man. One may also point to all the times the Nobel Committee abstained from awarding a Prize (sixteen times in the course of the period 1901–1960) in spite of the fact that often there were very competent women among the nominees.

It is, however, the language, argumentation, and forms of presentation in the evaluation reports that suggest that somewhat different criteria came into play when presenting the male and female candidates. The men's appearance, their civilian status, or their number of children are never mentioned. But for the women, such "vital statistics" are often in place. There are comments about Alexandra Kollontay's beauty and tight-fitting dresses, about Eleanor Roosevelt's many children, and about other women's lack of both husband and offspring.

It appears as though the women candidates are not judged on the basis of what they have achieved in their various areas of competence, but according to criteria from the men's world. However, given the very different backgrounds of the women and their limited possibilities for action in the public sphere, the female candidates were obviously unable to "compete" with the men on an equal footing.

MAIN CHARACTERISTICS OF MALE PRIZE LAUREATES

The male laureates generally came from prominent positions in organizational work, public administration, or politics. These positions became their springboard to recognition and fame in other areas and, recruitment to, for instance, leading

roles in the peace movement. Precisely because they were famous, their utterances about war and peace were noticed and
carried extra weight. Henri Dunant, René Cassin, Lord Boyd-
Orr, and Norway's own Fridtjof Nansen were all men who
became engaged in peace work as an extension of their roles
in areas that had made them highly visible in the public arena.

Politicians and state leaders constituted a significant group
of candidates for and recipients of the Nobel Peace Prize during
the course of the first decades of the twentieth century. President
Theodore Roosevelt was the first state leader to win the Prize
for his efforts as a peacemaker when he became a laureate in
1906 after mediating between Japan and Russia. The second
was also an American, Secretary of State Elihu Root, who won
the Prize in 1912. During the inter-war period of 1919–1939,
there are also many examples of prominent politicians who, due
to just their political stature, had the opportunity to influence
international opinion and thus be perceived as peacemakers.
President Wilson, Swedish Prime Minister Hjalmar Branting,
and Britain's Austin Chamberlain are names that may be noted in this context. In addition, one could mention Germany's
Gustav Stresemann and France's Aristide Briand, who were
both foreign ministers when the received the Prize in 1926. As
Irwin Abrams has underscored: "Statesmen are able to make
a contribution to peace because of their office, not necessarily
because of personal qualities or any long-term commitment to
the cause."[1] Obviously, women were unable to compete with
men on these grounds as they still did not have voting rights in
many countries. Even in the countries where they could vote,
women were prevented by deep-rooted traditional norms from
recruitment to the decision-making bodies.

MAIN CHARACTERISTICS OF NOMINATED WOMEN

For women nominees, the situation was obviously very

different from that of the male candidates for the Nobel Prize. Only Alexandra Kollontay had served in prominent political positions. Eleanor Roosevelt certainly enjoyed political influence, but had never held elective or paid political office. The same was true of Eva Peron.

Peace work had for many of the women candidates been their most absorbing interest. They had often dug deep in their own pockets and used personal economic resources to finance this work, which thus cost them a great deal, both literally and with regard to their reputations. As we have seen, Emily Greene Balch lost her position as professor at Wellesley College because of her peace activism. Both her work for peace and her socialist convictions were perceived as support for "the Reds" in a United States dominated by an almost hysterical fear of communism.

Peace activism became practically the main occupation of both Addams and Balch after the First World War. The same held true for Rosika Schwimmer and Elsa Brändström. Dedication to peace and hatred of war were the motivations behind all their work. It is also worth recalling that these women were among the first to launch the idea of an international peacekeeping organization, a league of nations. Mary Shapard, Jane Addams, and Rosika Schwimmer were the forerunners who articulated the demands that WILPF, the Women's International League for Peace and Freedom, later adopted and which Woodrow Wilson eventually received credit for—and a Peace Prize.

For many of the women Nobel Prize candidates, their peace activism had grown directly from their feminist engagement and their intense desire to improve the rights of women. Rosika Schwimmer, Lucia Ames Mead, Belva Ann Lockwood, and Carrie Chapman Catt were all active in the feminist movement before joining the peace movement. However, feminist organizational work did not have very high status in the eyes of the Nobel Committee consultants. We see this very clearly in the remark concerning Lady Aberdeen's candidature; it is a clear dismissal of her work and influence when the consultant points out that most of her supporters were women.

Besides being committed feminists, a great many of the thirty-six women described here were decidedly radical people. Feminism was of course in itself seen as extremely radical. In addition, when the women admitted socialist sympathies and demanded reforms in a male-dominated and capitalistic society, it is not hard to understand why they were perceived by their contemporaries not just as unrealistic utopians, but also as dangerous saboteurs of the social order.

The feminist revolution of the most recent decades has contributed to freeing women from the shackles imposed by yesterday's traditional societies, and as women increasingly are found in visible social positions, exercising influence and power, their numbers among Nobel candidates and Prize winners have also increased.

CONTROVERSIAL CANDIDATES

During the first half of the twentieth century, the Nobel Committee's reluctance to consider so-called "controversial candidates" as Prize recipients may likely have prevented the evaluation of women known to be political activists, such as Annie Besant and Rosika Schwimmer. The tradition, of course, might also exclude male candidates. Thus, Burton Feldman writes that the failure to give the Nobel Peace Prize to Mahatma Gandhi, even though he was nominated several times and enjoyed huge support, was probably due to his controversial political activism within his own country at a time when the Nobel Committee still regarded it as illegitimate to support nationalistic peace movements directed against the colonial powers.[2]

When the Peace Prize for 1960 was awarded to Albert Lutuli from South Africa, it represented a breach with this tradition, and since then there have been several awards to highly controversial candidates. Had the reasons for not awarding the Prize to a "controversial" Annie Besant been adhered to by the Nobel Committee when evaluating some of the candidates in more recent years, it is unlikely that Andrej Sakharov, Martin Luther King, or Aung San Suu Kyi would have received their awards. The same would apply to Bishop Tutu, Nelson Mandela, and the Dalai Lama. The motive behind awarding the Prize to these candidates and others like them who were at the center of ongoing conflicts and perceived as controversial and provocative, was the hope that the Peace Prize itself would influence the process toward peace, even though such an outcome might be far from certain.

Dr. Linus Pauling (Peace Prize laureate in 1962) said in a conversation with Irwin Abrams that obtaining this Prize might be especially important for dissidents to be able to continue their work. Abrams writes:

> The Nobel Peace Prize has been particularly important for dissidents at odds with their own governments. Linus Pauling, who had been refused a passport by the State Department because of his peace activities, said to me that winning the Nobel Prize made working for peace respectable: "Its effect was not so much on me and my actions, but on my reputation with the American people, who realized that what I said was in the interests of the United States and not just the Soviet Union.[3]

Several of the women who have been awarded the Nobel Peace Prize during the most recent years will surely support this statement. Controversial in their own countries because of their brave opposition to suppressive regimes and their support for human rights, Shirin Ebadi, Leymah Gbowee, and Tawakkol Karman have most certainly experienced that the Peace Prize has conferred on them a degree of security they would have missed without it.

THE ENLARGED CONCEPT OF PEACE

Over the course of the last decades, the Nobel Committee gradually appears to have redefined the concept of "work for peace" in a way that has broadened the groups of eligible recipients of the Peace Prize. According to Nobel's will, the Prize should go to people who had worked for the brotherhood of men, for demilitarization and reduction of armies, and who had been contributing to the arrangements of peace conferences. Already in 1901, the instruction was set aside: Henri Dunant, founder of the Red Cross, got the Prize for his work for the victims of war, not for having worked for peace. Most of the Nobel Prizes awarded up to the time of World War II did, however, adhere to the criteria stipulated by Alfred Nobel.

However, after 1945 the Nobel Committee has increasingly chosen to base its decisions on what may be called an "enlarged concept of peace." The Prize has gone to many people and organizations who have not been directly active in the work for peace and demilitarization, but who have contributed to eliminating the causes of conflict and social unrest, such as poverty, hunger, abuse of human rights, and lack of equality. By giving the Nobel Prize to John Boyd Orr in 1949 and to Norman Borlaug in 1970, the Nobel Committee signaled that it regarded it as peace building to eliminate the causes of human misery, which may also be the causes of war.

When Wangari Maathai received the Peace Prize in 2004, this enlarged concept of peace was expanded even further. For the first time ever, a Peace Prize candidate got the award for environmental work. Mathaai commented on her Prize by saying she believed the Nobel Committee had looked at the causes of war and seen what could be done to prevent conflict. A sustainable development with regard to the use of natural resources would further peace, she maintained.[4] The prize to Albert Gore and the UN Climate Panel three years later, in 2007, underscored again the view of the Nobel Committee: Ecological balance is an essential premise for peace.

Not everyone, however, is enthusiastic about this development. One of its strongest opponents is Norwegian lawyer Fredrik S. Heffermehl, who in several articles and books has criticized the Nobel Committee for its decisions. In his book *Nobels vilje,*[5] he argues that in several instances, and particularly after World War II, the Nobel Committee has completely ignored Alfred Nobel's instructions in his will with regard to the criteria for choosing the Prize recipients. The Committee has enlarged the concept of peace in an unacceptable way, says Heffermehl, and passed over Nobel's clear conditions, namely that the Peace Prize should be a reward to those who have made a contribution to the cause of international brotherhood, to demilitarization, and to the organizing of peace conferences.

Heffermehl distinguishes between what he describes as legitimate Peace Prizes, those that conform to Nobel's intentions as stated in his will, and "Committee Prizes," the results of the Nobel Committee's deviation from the intentions of the grantor or prizes that were given for something other than direct peace work. Humanitarian work; conciliation efforts in various conflict situations; work for women's equality; work toward a more just distribution of the world's resources; increased welfare and education for children—these are all good and worthy causes that deserve support. Still, they do not deserve a Nobel Prize, for the simple reason that Nobel's will stipulated other criteria for awarding the Prize.

The three women who received the Nobel Peace Prize during the period 1901–1960, von Suttner, Addams, and Greene

Balch, were undoubtedly "legitimate winners." But several of the other female nominees during these years were also well qualified with regard to precisely the criteria Heffermehl accuses the Committee of setting aside too many times. Especially before and during the First World War as well as during the inter-war period, women were, as we have seen, very active in the movement for demilitarization, mediation of international conflicts, and arranging peace conferences. WILPF and its leadership may certainly be characterized as the most active peace organization both before and after the Second World War and was nominated for the Nobel Peace Prize three times during the 1950s.

It appears curious that, during the years from 1901 until 1960, the Nobel Committee abstained from appointing a Prize winner sixteen times altogether, although there certainly were many qualified women among the nominees: Belva Ann Lockwood in 1914, Jane Addams in 1916, Rosika Schwimmer in 1917 and 1948, Elsa Brändström in 1923, 1924, and 1928, Lady Aberdeen in 1932, Carrie Chapman Catt in 1939, Eleanor Roosevelt in 1955, and Gertrude Baer and Margaret Sanger in 1956. Since the women were not considered even in years when there apparently were no male "rivals," it is hard to avoid a sneaking suspicion that there existed a general condescension among the Committee members toward women's contributions to the peace movement.

It has been maintained by some that because of the wars, it was impossible for the Nobel Committee to award prizes during these years. This is, however, incorrect. There are no rules that prevent the Committee from appointing winners during war time, and indeed, many prizes have been awarded while heated conflicts have been going on. Le Duc Tho and Henry Kissinger were honored in 1973 (Le Duc Tho refused to accept the Prize), two years before the Viet Nam war was over. And there certainly was no peace in the Middle East when Menachem Begin and

Anwar al-Sadat shared the Prize in 1978.

One may wonder, however, whether it was not the very narrow view of what constituted peace-related work that barred women from being considered seriously as candidates by the Nobel Committee. The strict interpretation of Nobel's will has perhaps hindered women's chances to be nominated during the first six decades of the Nobel Prize history. Men, not women, occupied positions that "naturally" led to leading roles in society. As statesmen, politicians, and prominent persons in organizational life, they were in the limelight and obtained the aura needed for even more honor and promotion. The women's arena—humanitarian and social work, responsibility for new generations and the old and sick, attention to human rights— was relegated to the background.

The gradual acceptance of an enlarged concept of peace work and increasing feminist consciousness have contributed to important social and cultural changes. Women's fight for a more child-friendly education and less authoritarian up- bringing of children slowly began to be seen as a pioneering contribution to the creation of a more peaceful society. The nomination of Lady Baden-Powell as a Peace Prize candidate may certainly be seen in this perspective. As "Chief Guide of the World," she was perceived as a major factor in the building of attitudes essential to peace. Margaret Sanger's work for fam- ily planning and Carrie Chapman Catt's revolutionary feminist message linked the dream of women's freedom to the dream of a more peaceful world, as did Maria Montessori's work. The nominations and the Prizes awarded to so many women during the years since 1975 indicate that it is against this background one finds the peace-related work that inspires hope of a less conflict-ridden world.

It is a curious consequence of Fredrik S. Heffermehl's strict definition of what constitutes a "legitimate" Nobel Prize that he regards most of the Prizes given to women between 1976 and

2004, six out of nine, as "Committee Prizes," in other words, as illegitimate. Only Alva Myrdal, Aung San Suu Kyi, and Jody Williams are accepted by him as "legitimate" winners. But the "Irish Peace Women," Mairead Corrigan and Betty Williams, Mother Teresa, Rigoberta Menchú Tum, Shirin Ebadi, and Wangari Maathai—they did not represent what Nobel wanted. "Brave, impressive, and significant" women, but not the right kinds of peace activists according to Heffermehl.[6] True enough, they had all worked for equality and human rights, but this was not in itself sufficient to meet the clear criteria of Nobel.

This literal and fundamentalist interpretation of Nobel's will, which means that many women Peace laureates are un- worthy winners in spite of their undisputed and important contributions toward creating the conditions required for peace to grow, does not appear convincing. Suggestions that the Nobel Committee should be "punished" for its "wrongdo- ings" have not led to more than soft-spoken debate in a narrow circle. Most likely the "enlarged peace concept" will continue to be employed and will thus allow people who have not been directly active against militarization or as sponsors of peace conferences to be recipients of the Nobel Peace Prize. The pow- erful secretary of the Nobel Committee for twenty-five years (1979–2014), history professor Geir Lundestad, has repeatedly stressed his conviction that it is essential to interpret Nobel's will in such a way that it is relevant to the modern world and not frozen in the context of the situation that existed a century ago.

A final factor worth noting regarding the Nobel Committee's view of women nominees is the Committee's composition. The five members are appointed by the Storting, the Norwegian parliament, after the various parties have pre- sented their candidates. The relative strength of the parties in the legislature determines who is finally selected. Before 1949, only men were appointed, but that year the Labor party's Aase

Lionæs, one of its most experienced politicians, got a seat on the Committee. She remained there for thirty years, the last ten years as leader of the Committee. All that time, however, she was the lone woman of the group—except when occasionally a female deputy member might have to step in because one of the permanent members was unable to attend. Not until the middle of the 1970s did the feminist Aase Lionæs manage to persuade the rest of the Committee that women should be seriously considered as Nobel laureates. The Irish "peace women," Mairead Corrigan and Betty Williams, received the awards for 1976.

Toward the end of the twentieth century more women were appointed members of the Nobel Committee, and from 2000 to the present, women have constituted a majority of the Committee members. The number of female laureates has increased. Considering the strong consciousness in Norway regarding the importance of women's representation in both public and private decision-making forums, it is not likely that female nominees will be discriminated or overlooked in the years ahead. On the contrary, there is every reason to believe that the trend toward more women among the laureates will increase.

In an article about women Nobel laureates during the twentieth century, Irwin Abrams hails the women for the ideals they shared and for their willingness to work and sacrifice in order to realize these ideals. He concludes by saying that they most surely were convinced that their goals would be achieved.[7] The first part of this statement certainly applies to all of the women nominated between 1901 and 1960, including the thirty-three who received no award. They were an impressive group of people, knowledgeable, idealistic, and hardworking. Many of them spent a lot of their time and resources promoting the cause of peace. But were they truly convinced that their goals would be achieved? I wonder. Surely, many must have been deeply disappointed over how seldom the world's politicians were moved to make decisions that would serve the cause of peace. Also, they must have fretted and grieved over how little their own hard work apparently influenced the development toward a civilized world order.

In the case of most of these courageous pioneers, their names have disappeared into the fog of history's forgetfulness. A few are remembered not for their peace work but for their contributions in other areas, as is the case for example of Maria Montessori. Hopefully, the day will come when the world will recognize its indebtedness to all of these women for how their selfless work in so-called "feminine areas" has contributed to creating the attitudes necessary to shape and sustain a peaceful world. They all deserve to be remembered, not forgotten.

Appendix A:
Female Peace Prize
Laureates 1976–2020

There is a substantial amount of literature about the thirteen women who have received the Peace Prize since 1976. Here I just present a few short notes, which for the most part are based on the works of Stenersen et al., 2001, 2009, and 2012. The comments on Malala Yousafzai are based on the information bulletin from the Nobel Institute in 2014 and Malala Yousafzai's Nobel lecture, printed in *Aftenposten*, December 11, 2014.

1976: Mairead Corrigan and
Betty Williams (The Irish Peace Women)

Mairead Corrigan (1944–) and Betty Williams (1943–) have been called "two quite ordinary housewives from Belfast." In their "ordinariness" they stood apart from most of the earlier women Prize winners. They had very little formal schooling and only modest experience in politics or organizational life. Even so, these two anonymous women managed to create a movement, which, in the course of a few months, made their names known all over the world.

The conflict between Protestants and Catholics in Northern Ireland had taken thousands of lives through centuries and seemed never to come to an end. In August 1976, three children were killed in a tragic accident: The driver of a car was shot by someone in the crowd, lost control of the vehicle, and killed the youngsters as the car careened to the side. The tragedy led Betty Williams to start a campaign against the meaningless and never-ending terror. Through newspapers, radio, and television, she appealed to people to join her in the work for peace. The aunt of the three dead children, Mairead Corrigan, contacted her, and together the two women became the leaders of a popular uprising, a peace movement based on nonviolence. In the course of less than a month, over 4,000 Irish men and women, old and young, Catholics and Protestants joined in a demonstration for peace. At first, they labeled themselves "Women for Peace," but shortly changed their name to the more inclusive "Community of Peace People." Already by the fall of 1976, the movement received massive support, international attention, and financial contributions from both the United States and European countries. Williams and Corrigan's names were more and more frequently mentioned in the debate concerning the year's Prize winners.

When the Nobel Committee postponed the decision regarding the Peace award for 1976, a spontaneous reaction occurred in Norway: Large sums of money were collected for a "People's Peace Prize," which was then handed over to the two women. This may have influenced the Nobel Committee, which in 1977 decided to award the Prize for 1976 to Williams and Corrigan.

As has so often happened, it turned out that the award was not greeted with unanimous support in the Prize winners' homeland. Criticism from both Catholic and Protestant quarters led Williams and Corrigan to withdraw as leaders of the peace movement, which by and by shriveled to a small core of only a few hundred members. In spite of this, one must not lose sight of the fact that it was the courageous initiative of

Williams and Corrigan that laid the basis for the peace process in Northern Ireland, a process that eventually resulted in formal peace agreements that have given the country a degree of stability that stands in stark contrast to the bloody past.

1979: Mother Teresa (1910–1997)

In 1928, an Albanian teenager, Agnes Gonsha Bojasihu, set out on a journey to India where she wanted to dedicate her life to help the poor. Already as a little girl, Agnes had felt a religious calling to serve those lowest on the steps of the social ladder, and as a teenager she decided to live and work in India. Following a relatively short stay in an Irish convent, she traveled to India and, at the age of 21, she became a nun and took the name Teresa. For the next two decades she taught at a girls' school in Calcutta, where she eventually became headmistress. However, this was far from a school for Calcutta's poor kids; on the contrary, its pupils were the offspring of India's "aristocracy"—the privileged high castes.

Teresa could not let go of her dream to come to the aid of the most poverty-stricken and ended up leaving the convent school in favor of teaching kids in the slum areas. She also started to work among the dying poor in the slums, and in 1950, she founded the Catholic order Missionaries of Charity, which reported directly to the Vatican. This order gradually spread across the globe, and schools for orphans were established in many countries as well as hospices for the dying.

"Mother Teresa" attained international fame in 1969 when BBC reporter Malcolm Muggeridge made a documentary about her work. Shortly, global attention led to prizes and awards of various kinds, and in 1972, the Canadian Prime Minister, Lester Pearson, nominated her for the Nobel Peace Prize. Three years later, in 1975, Senator Edward Kennedy was among those who proposed her name to the Nobel Committee.

The nominations resulted in masses of letters to the Committee expressing support for her candidature. When she finally won the Nobel Peace Prize in 1979, the Committee's decision was generally met with praise.

Teresa also had her critics. Most well known among them was perhaps journalist Christopher Hitchens, who during the 1990s attacked her both on television and in writing as a spokesperson for the most conservative forces inside the Catholic Church. Her views regarding family planning and abortion were especially subjected to harsh criticism.

Teresa had never been involved in any traditional type of peace activism. Clearly, the award of the Nobel Peace Prize to her was an example of the "enlarged peace concept" being employed to include humanitarian work on a large scale. Her great appeal may also have been due to the fact that she was perceived as a woman performing the typical female role—that of unselfishly aiding others. Her qualities as an astute business woman directing a global enterprise were hardly what commended her to her supporters.

1982: ALVA MYRDAL (1902–1986)

Swedish social reformer, politician, diplomat, and peace activist, Alva Myrdal received the Nobel Peace Prize in 1982. She was certainly a Prize winner who satisfied Alfred Nobel's demands as stated in his will; through a long life, she had indeed worked for the brotherhood of man and disarmament and been an active participant in the peace movement. She had already received prestigious prizes for her work: Albert Einstein's Peace Prize in 1980 and, two years later on the occasion of her 80th birthday, the Norwegian People's Peace Prize in recognition of her lifelong contribution to the international peace movement. Many were critical of the Nobel Committee for its decision that she had to share the Prize with a man, Alfonso Garcia Robles from Mexico.

Alva Reiner was meant to take over the family farm in Sweden, and her father insisted it was completely unnecessary to waste money on education for a future farmer. Alva was of another opinion—she studied on her own and passed all the high school exams necessary to go on to university studies. After completing her studies in Sweden, she took advanced courses in Great Britain, Germany, and Switzerland. She soon married her boyfriend from their teenage years, and together she and Gunnar Myrdal played an extremely important role in the development of the Swedish social welfare state during the inter-war period and the years following the Second World War.

After serving as Sweden's ambassador to India from 1955 to 1961, Alva Myrdal won a seat in the Riksdag in 1962, representing the Social Democrats. Four years later she accepted the post of disarmaments minister in Olof Palme's government, a position she held from 1966 to 1973. Both as a cabinet minister and as leader of Sweden's delegation to the Geneva talks on disarmament, she played an important part in the political deliberations. She had also represented Sweden at ILO and UNESCO meetings, and at the invitation of UN's Secretary Trygve Lie to become the head of the UN Department of Social Affairs, she served in that position in 1949–1950.[1] During the last years of her life, Alva Myrdal was especially active in the movement to reach an international agreement banning nuclear weapons and insisted that the European countries should declare Europe as a nuclear free zone. Both as a public speaker and the author of numerous books and articles, she warned against spiraling armaments and their enormous dangers, imploring politicians and ordinary citizens to join the movement for total rejection of atomic weapons.[2]

1991: AUNG SAN SUU KYI (1945–)

Aung San Suu Kyi is the only daughter of Burma's national hero, Aung San, who was murdered in 1947 by political rivals a couple of years before the fight he had led for Burmese independence from Great Britain was crowned with success. Suu Kyi's mother, Khin Kyi, was also a well-known and respected politician, who in 1960 became the Burmese ambassador to India. Thus, Suu Kyi's formative teenage years were spent as a school girl in New Delhi, where she got acquainted with Mahatma Gandhi's theory of nonviolence. It had a deep impact on her character and, in many ways, determined her own course and critical choices later on.

Only nineteen years old, Suu Kyi took off for England and social studies at Oxford University. After completing her bachelor degree, she went to New York where she worked at the United Nations for a few years before marrying her English fiancé, Professor Michael Aris, and returning to Europe in 1972. Two sons were born, and the young couple probably looked forward to a relatively quiet and retiring life in academia. However, in 1988, the family's situation altered dramatically when Suu Kyi's mother became ill. Aung San Suu Kyi went home to Burma to take care of her. Almost a quarter of a century was to pass before she was able to return to Europe.

The Burmese opposition party, the National League for Democracy (NLD), was founded in 1988 with Aung San Suu Kyi as a very engaged participant. At the national election two years later, the party she helped found won a decisive victory. It was, however, to no avail—the ruling military junta refused to hand over power, and Aung San Suu Kyi, NLD's most prominent leader and the one person most feared by the dictators, was placed under house arrest.

The regime's attempts to silence Suu Kyi had the opposite of the desired effect: Her reputation and popularity both at home and abroad grew, and she became the very symbol of the effectiveness of nonviolent resistance even against repressive military might. International prizes, such as the Norwegian Thorolf Rafto Memorial Award in 1990, the Sakharov Prize from the European Parliament in 1991, and finally the Nobel Peace Prize later that same year, all led to more and more nations imposing strong sanctions against the Burmese government. Gradually, international pressure contributed to the regime's cautious steps toward democratic reforms.

As a consequence of this hopeful development, Aung San Suu Kyi was finally able, twenty-one years after the award of the Peace Prize, to travel to Norway and deliver her Nobel Lecture at Oslo City Hall on June 16, 2012. Millions of television spectators watched and listened with rapt attention as the slender, ramrod straight woman who had defied her country's military rulers for so many years, gave her account of the development toward democracy in one of the world's most closed political systems.

Regarding the reasons for awarding the Peace Prize to Aung San Suu Kyi in 1991, the Nobel Committee chairman, Professor Francis Sejersted, said that the Committee considered her as a symbol of "the good fight for peace and reconciliation" and admired her respect for human rights.[3] It is a somewhat ironic commentary on the very real role of realism and pragmatism in politics when Suu Kyi, today a free and active political leader in a Burma taking its tentative steps toward realizing democracy, has not been willing or able to support the quest of the country's persecuted and suppressed Muslim minority, the Rohingya, that *their* human rights be respected. The overwhelming victory of her party in the November 8, 2015 elections gave hope that she would be able to include Burma's disfranchised minorities on the agenda confronting Burma's new regime, but this has unfortunately not happened. On the contrary, Aung San Suu Kyi has ruined her legacy through her continued support for the regime's oppressive policies toward the Rohingya.

1992: RIGOBERTA MENCHÚ TUM (1959–)

At only 33 years of age, Rigoberta Menchú Tum from Guatemala was the youngest Prize laureate up to then when she received the Nobel Peace Prize in 1992. She was also the first native Indian woman to become a Nobel laureate, and as Atle Sveen points out, her award "was interpreted as a mark of recognition to the Indian population of Guatemala and the American continent and to the indigenous populations of the world."[4] Unlike most of the other female candidates for the Prize, Roberta Menchú Tum had grown up in severe poverty, received very little education, and had to leave home when she was twelve in order to work as a housemaid. However, her parents were politically conscious people, and as a child Roberta often went with her father on his trips around the country as a political agitator, attempting to organize the terribly poor indigenous people of Guatemala into an effective opposition against the suppressive regime. When Rigoberta was 21, her father was killed by the army. Her mother was arrested and died of mistreatment suffered in jail, and one of her brothers was publicly executed by the military.

Rigoberta herself was early identified as a dangerous threat to the regime because of her activity among poor peasants and industrial workers. She sought refuge in Mexico, where she established contact with political activists who supported her struggle against the dictatorship in her home country. Before the age of 25, she became internationally know when her autobiography, *I, Rigoberta Menchú,* was published in 1983.

The superior military strength of the regime in power caused Roberta to review and change her strategies. Rather than fighting the government, she assumed the role of mediator between the guerrillas and the regime. During a trip to Europe, she had met influential politicians, among them Norway's parliamentarian Inger-Lise Gjørv, who nominated Roberta for the Nobel Peace Prize. The earlier Prize recipient, Bishop Desmond Tutu, also proposed her as a candidate, and when Guatemala hosted a conference of the world's aborigines in 1991, the conference decided to support her for the Prize.

The Norwegian government resolved to act as a mediator between the guerrillas and the Guatemalan government, and in 1996, four years after Rigoberta received her award in Oslo City Hall, a peace treaty was signed in the war-ridden country.

1997: Jody Williams (1950–)

A native of Vermont, Jody Williams received the Nobel Peace Prize in 1997, the third American woman to become a Nobel laureate.

Williams got the award for her leadership in the battle against landmines. As a student at the University of Vermont and Johns Hopkins School of Advanced International Studies where she obtained degrees in psychology and international relations, Jody Williams had become keenly aware of the enormous injuries and sufferings sustained by the victims of landmines. As a student she had participated in humanitarian work in El Salvador and had personally seen how these weapons ruined the lives of both children and adults. After completing her studies, Jody worked for some time for various nongovernmental organizations (NGOs) before joining the president of the Vietnam Veterans of America Foundation, Robert Muller, and a few other political activists, in a decision to start a campaign against landmines.

Jody agreed to accept the position as leader of the International Campaign to Ban Landmines (ICBL). She proved to be an exceptionally skilled organizer, and ICBL saw a rapid increase in its following. At the international conference held in Canada in 1996, there were participants from about fifty nations and observers from many more. The Canadian Secretary of Foreign Affairs, Lloyd Axworthy, was particularly active and won support for his proposal that another conference be held the following year for the purpose of signing a convention against landmines. At the conference in 1997, the agreement to forbid production, sale, store, and use of landmines was signed by 120 states. By March 1999, over forty countries had ratified the agreement, which then became binding as international law. The politicians in Jody Williams's own country, however, refused to ratify the treaty, and President Bill Clinton was not among those sending congratulations when Williams received the Nobel Prize for her work for peace and disarmament.

2003: SHIRIN EBADI (1947–)

Iranian lawyer and human rights activist Shirin Ebadi was the first Muslim woman to receive the Nobel Peace Prize. Ebadi grew up in a well-to-do family where liberal and tolerant attitudes dominated the home. Her father was an ardent supporter of Mohammad Mosaddegh and the democratic reform program that Mosaddegh pursued after he became prime minister in 1951. Ebadi's father served as Agriculture Vice Minister in Mosaddegh's government, but his career came to an abrupt end in 1953 when the CIA-supported coup in Iran felled the democratically elected government of Mosaddegh.

Shirin Ebadi was only six years old when this fateful political drama occurred, but she still recalls the moment when the family was listening to the radio news, and she saw the sombre faces of the adults, she reports in her book *Iran Awakening*.[5] As a little girl and young student, she identified with the Iranian opposition, and when the revolution started in 1978, it was a matter of course for her to join the revolutionaries in their battle against the hated regime of the Shah. In her book she reminisces about the joy she felt when the revolution succeeded, and then the enormous disappointment that soon set in:

> That day I experienced a wave of pride, something I now, later laugh at. I felt that I too, had won, together with this victorious revolution. Hardly a month passed before I realized that I had, in fact, with will and enthusiasm participated in my own ruin. I was a woman, and this revolution demanded my defeat.[6]

In 1970, Shirin Ebadi had completed her university law studies at the top of her class, and five years later, as the first Iranian woman ever, she was appointed judge of the city court of Tehran. However, the revolution that she had supported so eagerly meant the end of her career. As a woman she was not competent to be a judge according to the religious leaders of the country, and she was demoted to a position as office clerk. She also lost her license to practice as a lawyer. Shirin decided to resign from her job as a clerk and launched a freelance career as a writer and lecturer, focusing on family law reform and humanitarian rights, especially the rights of women and children. In 1994, she was among the founders of the Society for Protecting the Rights of the Child (SPRC), intended to make sure that the UN Children's Convention, which Iran had signed, would be enforced.

When her lawyer's license was restored in 1992, Shirin Ebadi opened her own law office. She soon realized that the Iranian legal system was so corrupt that only by working for free, not demanding any fees for her legal services, would she be able to function. The Nobel Peace Prize in 2003 was particularly an award for her unselfish aid to women and children as well as minority groups who were the victims of Iran's unjust legal system, but the Nobel Committee also noted her unflagging support for the principle that "the supreme political power in a community must be built on democratic elections" as well as her belief in "enlightenment and dialogue as the best path to changing attitudes and resolving conflicts."[7]

2004: WANGARI MAATHAI (1940–2011)

The first African woman to receive the Nobel Peace Prize was Kenya'sWangari Maathai. She was born in Nyeri, north of Nairobi, and unlike most girls in Kenya at the time, she received a very good education. After finishing basic schooling in Kenya, she went to the United States where she earned her bachelor of science degree in Kansas and then a master of science at the University of Pittsburgh in Pennsylvania. When she returned home, she continued her studies and obtained her doctoral degree in 1971—the first woman in Kenya to receive a doctoral degree. She was also Kenya's first female professor when she was appointed as a professor at the University of Nairobi.

As a researcher, Mathaai was intensely concerned about the catastrophic deforestation occurring in large parts of Africa; in Kenya alone, 90 percent of the forest was lost during the decades from 1950 to 2000. In 1977, Wangari Maathai decided to resign from her position at the university in order to devote all her time to the organization she had launched, the Green Belt Movement, which would battle deforestation through systematic tree planting.

However, the Green Belt Movement also led to conflict, both with foreign investors and politicians in her own country, and Wangari Maathai had to endure both legal trials and time in jail. But the attention she received also made her name steadily better known, and in 2002 she decided to compete for a seat in the parliament. President Arap Moi lost the election, while Maathai started her career as a full-time politician. The following year she was appointed assistant minister for Environment, Natural Resources, and Wildlife.

Ole Danbolt Mjøs, the leader of the Nobel Committee, said

in his speech at the award ceremony that the Committee now had expanded the basis for the award and had accepted work for environmental protection as furthering the cause of peace. As Asle Sveen points out, this expansion of the concept of peace is a logical consequence of the path already chosen by the Committee when it presented the Peace Prize to John Boyd Orr in 1949 and to Norman Borlaug in 1960: Both of these men, he writes, "believed that hunger and need were fundamental causes of conflict, and that finding ways to increase global food production would also serve to prevent war."[8] Wangari Maathai expressed the same conviction in her speech thanking for the Prize: "I think what the Nobel Committee is doing is going beyond war and looking at what humanity can do to prevent war. Sustainable management of our natural resources will promote peace."[9]

2011: ELLEN JOHNSON SIRLEAF (1938–)

For the very first time in the history of the Nobel Peace Prize, three women shared the prize for 2011. They were Africa's first female president, Ellen Johnson Sirleaf, her fellow coun-try-woman, Leymah Gbowee, and Yemen's Tawakkol Karman. The awards represented a resounding support for women's nonviolent struggle for peace in Africa and the Middle East.

Ellen Johnson Sirleaf won the presidential election in Liberia in 2005, and her first big task was to get the country rebuilt after the devastating civil war that had been going on for many years, a task she succeeded in accomplishing.

Johnson Sirleaf has a solid education. Following econom-ics studies in Liberia, she continued her university education in the United States where she first studied in Wisconsin and then in Colorado before eventually obtaining her master's degree in public policy from the John F. Kennedy School of Government at Harvard University. After her return to Liberia she was appointed Minister of Finance, but served only one year (1979–1980) before she was forced into exile because of the military coup by Samuel Doe and his followers and the ensuing terror regime.

While in exile, Johnson Sirleaf worked for a while in international banking, but in 1992, she accepted a leading position at the United Nations with the responsibility for African development. She was also strongly interested in the effort to strengthen the position of African women, as well as recruiting them into active political participation.

In the 1989 presidential election, Charles Taylor decided to confront Samuel Doe, and civil war broke out once more. Ellen Johnson Sirleaf had first supported Taylor, but she was soon disappointed about his leadership when he came to power. She stood as a candidate for the presidency in the election of 1997, but sustained a severe loss, gaining less than 10 percent of the vote. She again decided to leave the country. However, when Charles Taylor was accused of war crimes, Ellen Johnson Sirleaf returned to Liberia and in 2005, she once more stood as a candidate for the presidency. This time she won a resounding victory.

The new president faced enormous challenges. The long and bloody civil war had demanded over 200,000 lives, a great number of people had fled, and the country's infrastructure was ruined. Even so, Johnson Sirleaf managed to obtain a peace treaty. Human rights legislation was adopted, and the president showed that she was concerned about women's rights in society. Schooling for girls and access for women to male-dominated occupations were placed on the agenda. In spite of criticism and accusations of corruption, "Grandmother" or "Old Ma," as she was often called, became popular in Liberia, especially among women. The country was finally at peace, and the economy began improving. International commentators praised her leadership, and a few days after accepting the Nobel Peace Prize for her nonviolent struggle for women's security and their right to full participation in society, Ellen Sirleaf won reelection and started her second period as president of Liberia.[10]

2011: Leymah Gbowee (1972–)

The other Liberian woman to receive the Nobel Peace Prize in 2011, Leymah Gbowee, had also been a major player in the country's political liberation from dictatorship. Like President Sirleaf, she was well educated, first trained as a crisis therapist in Nigeria and later achieving a master's degree in conflict management in the United States. During the civil war, she worked with youngsters who had been recruited as child soldiers and suffered from post-traumatic stress. Their reports of horrible war experiences contributed to her engagement for peace. Deeply religious and active in the Lutheran Church of Liberia, Leymah Gbowee decided to establish a multicultural women's opposition against the war with both Christian and Muslim women joining in an effective grassroots movement for peace. Gbowee's organizational skills and the women's demonstrations against Charles Taylor's government and wholehearted support for Sirleaf undoubtedly represented a significant contribution to Taylor's loss in the 2005 election and Ellen Sirleaf's return as president.

The 2008 prize-winning documentary film "Pray the Devil Back to Hell" features Leymah Gbowee in a starring role as herself; she tells the incredible story about the Liberian women's unconventional methods in "making war on war" and their fight for women's rights. The film helped make Leymah Gbowee internationally known and shows how nonviolent, untraditional modes of action may be effectively used in the movement for peace.

2011: TAWAKKOL KARMAN (1979–)

The third Peace Prize laureate in 2011, Tawakkol Karman from Yemen, was the youngest person until then who had been awarded the Peace Prize. She is also the first Arab woman to have won the Prize.

As the daughter of a politician (her father had been a member of the Yemenite government), Tawakkol became interested in politics at quite a young age. After completing her university education in social science studies, she started work as a journalist and joined the opposition party Al-Islah. She quickly became known as a sharp critic of the governing regime, and in particular, she was noted for her views regarding women's position in society and her many proposals for improving their situation.

An interest organization calling itself "Journalist Women Without Chains" was launched in 2005, and Tawakkol was one of the founders. From 2007 to 2010, this group staged weekly demonstrations demanding democratic reforms in the country.

In 2011, "The Arabic Spring" was felt in Yemen as well as in many other countries in the Middle East, with clamors for sociopolitical changes. As a leader of a growing reform movement, Tawakkol Karman flew to New York in an attempt to influence the U.N. Security Council to pass a resolution against Yemen's president Saleh's regime, charging him with crimes against human rights and requesting that he be prosecuted by the International Court of Criminal Justice. Although the United Nations passed a resolution condemning the president for his oppressive politics, no charges were lodged that would have placed him before the Court of Criminal Justice.

Tawakkol Karman became a great media favorite during her days in Oslo in connection with the Nobel festivities, but since then, she has been almost completely invisible. It remains to be seen whether she'll be able to lead the process of democratization in Yemen to lasting results. So far, it appears that the country's patriarchal regime has succeeded in silencing the opposition that Karman and her supporters represent, if not altogether destroying it.[11] The devastating civil war in Yemen has stopped the work for human rights.

2014: MALALA YOUSAFZAI (1997–)

The whole world knows Malala, the teenager who, on October 10, 2014, got the message from Oslo that she would be the sixteenth woman and the very youngest person to receive the Nobel Peace Prize, an award she would share with India's Kailash Satyarthi. The Nobel Committee press release declared that they would receive the Prize "for their struggle against oppression of children and young people and for the right of all children to education."

Malala Yousafzai grew up in the Swat Valley in Pakistan, and as a twelve-year-old child she became a strong spokesperson for young girls' right to education, getting known throughout the country for her passionate speeches, articles, and use of social media, arguing for women's rights. The Taliban, who enjoyed a strong position in the area, did not at all appreciate Malala's "impertinence." The young girl was warned that there would be serious consequences if she did not stop talking. Death threats started appearing, but Malala did not budge.

When neither warnings nor threats seemed to help, someone from the Taliban leadership decided to put a final stop to Malala exercising her right to speak her mind. On October 9, 2012, the school bus of which she was a passenger was stopped, and Malala was shot through the head. Miraculously, she survived and was rushed to Great Britain for surgery and a lengthy hospital stay. When she was fully recovered, she resumed her writing and public speaking and soon became an international symbol of girls' and women's rights to equality, as well as the fight against political extremism and fanaticism. Her sixteenth birthday was spent in New York, where she addressed the United Nations' General Assembly with a speech so forceful that it brought her worldwide praise for the courage she showed in attacking hypocrisy and oppression. President Barack Obama invited her to the White House, where she spoke out against the U.S. military's use of drones as a violation against human rights.

Kailash Satyarthi, who shared the Prize with Malala, commented on their award the day after it was announced: "The award has brought together a Pakistani and an Indian activist, a Hindu and a Muslim, a grown-up and a child, who in spite of great differences have a common cause they fight for." The Nobel Committee emphasized that the prize winners' work for children and youth contributes to realizing brotherhood among nations, thus meeting one of Alfred Nobel's criteria for receiving the prize.[12]

Geir Lundestad, who was then secretary of the Nobel Committee, sees the 2014 Prize award as an important extension of the enlarged concept of freedom: The Nobel Committee had long been supporting the fight for democracy and human rights, he says, but had seldom "broadened the perspective to include children and youth." The prize to Kailash Satyarthi and Malala Yousafzai rectified this, and was "an expression of a growing global conscience." In the words of the Committee: "Children shall go to school, not be exploited for economic purposes."[13]

2018: NADIA MURAD (1993–)

In 2018 a Yazidy woman from Iraq, Nadia Murad, shared the Nobel Peace Prize with the Congolese gynecologist, Dr. Denis Mukwege. The prize was a recognition of their "efforts to end the use of sexual violence as a weapon of war and armed conflict," said Berit Reiss-Andersen, leader of the Nobel Peace Prize Committee, when announcing the decision in Oslo on October 5, 2018. Nadia Murad was the seventeenth woman, the first Iraqi woman, as well as the first Yazidi, to earn the Nobel Peace Prize. She was also the next youngest female laureate ever, only 25 years old.

In her moving Nobel lecture, Murad described the contrast between an idyllic childhood and the events that led her to world fame. She was born into a large farming family in the small village Kojo in the Sinjar province in northern Iraq. Her dreams for the future were simple - finishing high school and then establishing a beauty parlor in her village, close to friends and relatives. "But this dream became a nightmare," she says, describing how the ISIS attacks in August of 2014 resulted in genocide of the Yazidy ethnic and cultural group to which she belongs. ISIS "tried to eradicate one of the components of Iraq by taking women into captivity, killing men and destroying our pilgrimage sites and houses of worship," she said.

During these atrocities, Murad lost her mother, six brothers and numerous nephews and nieces. "Every Yazidy family has a similar story, one more horrible than the other," she said. She ended up, along with many other Yazidi women, as a sex slave, subjected to horrendous torture and sexual abuse. After three months, she succeeded in escaping, eventually finding her way to a refugee camp. Through a refugee program, she eventually obtained a visa to Germany, where she now lives.

Rather than keeping silent about the horrors she and other Yazidy women experienced under ISIS rule, she wrote and spoke about the war crimes committed by the Islamic State. Her voice was heard, as she traveled all over the world, pleading the cause of the Yazidis and other persecuted minorities.

In 2016 she was named the first UN Goodwill Ambassador for the Dignity of Survivors of Human Trafficking. The same year she won the EU Parliamentarians' Sakharov Prize and the Vaclav Havel Prize for Human Rights from the European Council. With the Nobel Peace Prize two years later, she became a recognized name worldwide.[14]

When 17-year-old Malala Yousafzai became the youngest Peace Prize laureate in 2014, the secretary of the Nobel Committee at the time, Geir Lundestad, saw this as an important extension of the broadened concept of freedom. The prize was an expression of a growing global conscience, recognizing that freedom for children is the right to go to school. The Peace Prize to Nadia Murad and Denis Mukwege must be seen in the same perspective: a recognition of women's rights to own their own bodies.

Appendix B:
Women Nominated for the
Nobel Peace Prize (1901–1960)

Bertha von Suttner 1901, 02, 03, 04, 05. Shortlisted 1903, 04. Recipient 1905.

Belva Ann Lockwood 1901, 02, 14. Shortlisted 1914.

Priscilla Hanna Peckover 1903, 05, 11, 13. Shortlisted 1905, 13.

Henriette Verdier Winteler de Weindeck. 1905, 07, 10, 11.

Madame Angela de Oliveira Cezar de Costa 1910, 11.

Anna Eckstein 1913.

Lucia Mead 1913, shortlisted.

Jane Addams 1916, 23, 24, 25, 28, 29, 30, 31. Shortlisted in 1916, 23, 25, 31. Recipient in 1931.

Rosika Schwimmer 1917, 1948.

Mary Shapard 1919.

Madame Severine (Widow Guebhard) 1920, 22, 24, 27, 29.

Eglantyne Jebb 1922.

Elsa Brändström 1922, 23, 28, 29. Shortlisted 1928.

Lady Aberdeen 1931, 32, 34, 35, 36, 37. Shortlisted 1931, 32, 34.

Annie Besant 1931, shortlisted.

Princess Marguerite-Antoinette Heraclius Djabadary 1933. (The only woman among forty-seven nominees that year.

Juliet Bikle 1935, 36, 37.

Janet Miller 1935.

Irma Schweitzer 1936, 37.

Moina Michael 1936.

Henriette Szold 1937.

Princess Henriette of Belgium 1938.

Carrie Chapman Catt 1939, shortlisted. (Only woman among twenty nominees.)

Alexandra Kollontay 1946, 47. Shortlisted 1946.

Emily Greene Balch, recipient 1946.

Eleanor Roosevelt 1947, 49, 55, 59. Shortlisted 1947, 49, 59.

Katharine Bruce Glasier 1948.

Maria Montessori 1949, 50, 51.

Eva Peron 1949.

Princess Wilhelmina of Nederland (previously Queen Wilhelmina) 1951.

Dr. Elisabeth Rotten 1952, 56, 57, 59, 60.

Barbara Waylen 1952.

Margaret Sanger 1953, 54, 55, 56, 60. Shortlisted 1953, 60.

Helen Keller. 1954, 58. Shortlisted 1958.

Gertrude Baer 1955, 56, 57, 58, 59. Shortlisted 1955, 57.

Lady Baden-Powell 1959, shortlisted.

Appendix C: Tables

Table 1: Peace Prize Recipients 1901–1960

	1901–25	1926–50	1951–60	Total
Women	1	2	0	3
Men	23	16	7	46
Organizations	3	4	1	8
Total	27	22	8	57

Table 2: Peace Prize Recipients 1901–2020

	1901–1975	1976–2020*	Total
Men	57	33	90
Women	3	14	17
Organizations	12	16	28
Total	72	63	135

Appendix D:
Consultants Cited in the Text

Keilhau, Wilhelm

Koht, Halvdan

Lange, Christian L.

Lie, Mikael

Moe, Ragnvald

Munthe, Preben

Røed, Ole Thorleif

Schou, August

Seip, Jens Arup

Seyersted, Finn

Tønnesson, Kåre

Wold, Knut Getz

Endnotes

Introduction by the Author
1. Stenersen et al., 2001, p. 12

Chapter 1:
The Background for the Nobel Peace Prize
1. Heffermehl, 2008, p. 22.
2. Cited by Lundestad, 2015, p.14.
3. *The Nobel Peace Prize and the Laureates* (1988).
4. Ibid., p. 25.
5. Holl, Karl, and Anne C. Kjelling (eds.), 1994, p. 20.
6. Feldman, 2000, p. 327.

Chapter 2: The Period 1901–1940
1. Stenersen et al. 2001, p. 42.
2. Veseth, 2000, p. 25.
3. Stenersen, op. cit. p. 42.
4. Abrams, 1988, p. 28.
5. Stenersen et al. 2001, p. 110.
6. Abrams, op.cit. p. 122.
7. Ibid., p. 123.
8. Nobel Committee Report, 1916, p. 16.
9. Stenersen et al. p. 110.
10. NNK Report, 1905, pp. 58–59.
11. NNK Report, 1913, p. 48.

12. Craig, 1990, p. 71.
13. Ibid., p. 53.
14. Ibid.
15. Ibid., p. 95.
16. Craig, op. cit. p. 89.
17. Ibid., p. 88.
18. NNK Report, 1924, p. 32.
19. Norgren, 1999, p.18.
20. Norgren, 2002, p. 12.
21. NNK Report, 1914, p. 32.
22. Veseth, p. 11.
23. Anna B. Eckstein, Papers, 1886–1944, Swarthmore College Peace Collection.
24. Edith Wynner wrote *The Life and Times of Rosika Schwimmer,* but the manuscript was never published. It is part of the Schwimmer–Lloyd Collection papers at the New York Public Library.
25. Cited in *"Rosika Schwimmer, World Patriot: A Biographical Sketch,* 1947, p. 4, Schwimmer–Lloyd Collection papers, New York Public Library.
26. See the Nobel Peace Institute's copies of publications from the Schwimmer–Lloyd Collection at the New York Public Library.
27. Nobel Institute Archives, Mary Shapard's file, letter #9, 1919.
28. Ibid.
29. Nobel Peace Institute, Mary Shapard's file, "The Original Peace Movement," in *Free Lance,* 1917.
30. *Biographical Dictionary of Modern Peace Leaders* (p. 873).
31. Nobel Institute Archives, Jebb file, letter #15, 1922.
32. *Dagsavisen,* June 2, 2004.
33. NNK Report, 1928, p. 27.
34. Ibid., p. 28.

35. NNK Report, 1931, p. 14.

36. Ibid.

37. Ibid.

38. Nobel Institute Archives, Aberdeen file, letter # 59, 1935.

39. Ibid.

40. Nobel Institute Archives, Aberdeen file, letter #47, 1937.

41. NNK Report, 1931, p. 15.

42. Ibid., pp. 16–17.

43. Ibid.

44. Ibid.

45. Ibid., p. 18.

46. Nobel Institute Archives, Djabadary file, letter #70, 1933.

47. Nobel Institute Archives, Miller file, letters # 101,102, and 103, 1934. See also Jorja Frazier, "Little Brown Sparrow of a Woman: Dr. Janet Miller, Return to Elmwood," Spring 2011, www.elmwoodcemetery.org.

48. Nobel Institute Archives, Bikle file, letter #45, January 26, 1935.

49. Reprinted in *Badener Neujahrsblätte* (vol. 44, 1969).

50. Nobel Institute Archives, Szold file, letter #15, 1937.

51. Nobel Institute Archives, Princess Henriette's file, letter #53, 1937.

52. NNK Report, 1939, p. 23.

53. Ibid.

54. Ibid., p. 22.

55. Ibid., p. 24.

56. Ibid.

57. NNK Report, 1939, p. 25.

58. Ibid., p. 26.

CHAPTER 3:

THE POSTWAR PERIOD 1945–1960

1. NNK Report, 1946, p. 15.
2. Ibid., p. 14.
3. Ibid., p. 13.
4. Ibid., p. 24.
5. Holl/Kjelling, op.cit. p. 222.
6. NNK Report, 1946, p. 43.
7. Ibid., p. 44.
8. Ibid.
9. Ibid., p. 45.
10. Ibid., p. 46.
11. Ibid.
12. Ibid., p. 45.
13. Ibid., pp. 46–47.
14. NNK Report, 1946, p. 52.
15. See Lionæs, 1987, p. 43; also *Pax Leksikon* (Pax Encyclopedia), volume 3, "Kollontaj, Alexandra," pp. 442–444.
16. NNK Report, 1946, p. 53.
17. NNK Report, 1947, p. 57.
18. See Cook, II, p. 161.
19. Cook, II, p. 239.
20. NNK Report, 1947, p. 61.
21. Ibid., p. 64.
22. NNK Report, 1949, p. 46.
23. Ibid.
24. NNK Report, 1959, p. 63.
25. Ibid.
26. Linder, 1997, p. 224–27.
27. Abrams, p. 25.
28. Cited by Viseth, p. 141.
29. Bussey, 1965, p. 19.

30. NNK Report, 1955, p. 79.

31. NNK Report, 1955, p. 19.

32. Ibid., p. 20.

33. Ibid., p. 22.

34. Ibid., p. 24.

35. Nobel Institute Archives, Glasier file, letter #21, 1948.

36. Kramer, 1976, p. 22.

37. See her article in *Kvinnenes Kulturhistorie* (Women's Cultural History), II, p. 172.

38. Bodil Führ, *Aftenposten,* July 26, 2002.

39. Nobel Institute Archives, Wilhelmina file, #63, January 25, 1951, January 31, 1951.

40. Please also see Dutch historian Dr. Han van Bree, who in his Ph.D. dissertation included a chapter on Barbara Waylen's participation in a peace conference in the Netherlands in 1951. His dissertation was published in 2015 by Conserve, Schoorl. The title: "*De geest van het Oude-Loo. Juliana en haar vriendenkring 1947–1957*" (The spirit of the Oude-Loo. Juliana and her circle of friends from 1947 to 1957).

41. NNK Report, 1953, p. 62.

42. Ibid., p. 45.

43. Ibid.

44. NNK Report, 1960, p. 80.

45. See Gloria Steinem, "Margaret Sanger," *Time Magazine*, April 13, 1998.

46. NNK Report, 1958, p. 16.

47. Ibid., p. 17.

48. Ibid., p. 19.

49. NNK Report, 1959, p. 11.

50. Ibid., p. 14.

51. Ibid., p. 15.

CHAPTER 4: CONCLUSIONS

1. Abrams, 1988, p. 27.
2. Feldman, 2000, pp. 324–25.
3. Abrams, pp. 29–30.
4. See Stenersen et al., 2012, p. 15.
5. *Nobel's Will*, Oslo, 2008.
6. op. cit. p. 55.
7. "Fredens heltinner, ni av Nobels kvinner," Wikipedia.

APPENDICES: A–D

1. Stenersen et al., 2001, p. 227.
2. See Myrdal, *The Game of Disarmament,* 1978.
3. Stenersen et al., 2001, p. 254.
4. Stenersen et al., 2001, p. 256.
5. Ebadi, 2006, p. 19.
6. Ibid., p. 54.
7. Øyvind Stenersen, Stenersen et al., 2009, p. 10.
8. Stenersen et al., 2009, p. 13.
9. Ibid.
10. See Stenersen et al., op. cit. 2012, pp. 28–29, and Skard, 2012, pp. 310–317.
11. See Stenersen et al., 2012, p. 29.
12. *Aftenposten*, October 11, 2014, pp. 4–5.
13. Lundestad, 2015, p. 280.
14. Nobel Institute, press release, December 2018.

Archival Material

Anna B. Eckstein, Papers, 1886–1944, Swarthmore College Peace Collection.

Gro Brækken, *Dagsavisen,* June 2, 2004.

Nobel Committee Report, 1916, p. 16.

Nobel Institute Archive, Aberdeen file, letter # 59, 1935.

Nobel Institute Archives, Aberdeen file, letter #47, 1937.

Nobel Institute Archive, Bikle file, letter #45, January 26, 1935.

Nobel Institute Archives, Djabadary file, letter #70, 1933.

Nobel Institute Archives, Jebb file, letter #15, 1922.

Nobel Institute Archives, Mary Shapard file, letter #9, 1919.

Nobel Peace Institute, Mary Shapard's file, "The Original Peace Movement," in *Free Lance*, 1917.

Nobel Institute Archives, Miller file, letters # 101,102, and 103, 1934.

NNK Reports (Nobelkomiteens Rapporter), 1901–1960.

1905, pp. 58–59.

1913, p. 48.

1914, p. 32.

1924, p. 32.

1928, p. 27.

1931, p. 14.

1931, p. 15.

1931, pp. 16–17.

BIBLIOGRAPHY

Abrams, Irwin (1988): *The Nobel Peace Prize and the Laureates. An Illustrated Biographical History*, 1901–1987. Boston: Hall.

Alonso, Harriet Hyman (1994): "Jane Addams and Emily Greene Balch: The Two Women of WILPF," in Holl, Karl, and Anne C. Kjelling, (eds., 1994): *The Nobel Peace Prize and the Laureates*. Frankfurt am Main: Peter Lang.

Biographical Dictionary of Modern Peace Leaders (p. 873).

Bussey, Gertrude, and Margaret Tims (1965): *Pioneers for Peace. Women's International League for Peace and Freedom, 1915–1965*. London: George Allen & Unwin Ltd.

Cook, Blanche Wiesen (1992): *Eleanor Roosevelt*, Vol. 1, 1884–1933. New York: Viking.

Cook, Blanche Wiesen (1999): *Eleanor Roosevelt*, Vol. 2, 1933–1938. New York: Viking.

Craig, John M. (1990): "Lucia Ames Mead and the American Peace Movement (1856–1936)." *Studies in World Peace*, Vol. 4. The Edwin Mellen Press.

Ebadi, Shirin (2006): *Iran våkner*. Oslo: N.W. Damm & Søn.

Elster, Ellen (2007): "NATO, Beredskapslovene og selvpålagte restriksjoner." Oslo: Fred og frihet, jubileumsnummer.

Feldman, Burton (2000): *The Nobel Prize. A History of Genius, Controversy and Prestige.* New York: Arcade Publishing.

Fox, Mary Virginia (1975): *Lady for the Defense: A Biography of Belva Lockwood.* New York: Harcourt.

Heffermehl, Fredrik S. (2008): *Nobels vilje.* Oslo: Vidarforlaget.

Holl, Karl, and Anne C. Kjelling (eds., 1994): *The Nobel Peace Prize and the Laureates.* Frankfurt am Main: Peter Lang.

Josephson, Harold (ed., 1985): *Biographical Dictionary of Modern Peace Leaders.* Greenwood Press.

Kramer, Rita (1976): *Maria Montessori.* New York: G. P. Putnam's Sons.

Linder, Dorothy (1997): *Aase Lionæs. En politisk biografi.* Oslo: Det norske Arbeiderparti.

Lionæs, Aase (1987): *Tredveårskrigen for freden.* Høydepunkter i Nobelkomiteens historie (The thirty-year war for peace. Highlights in the history of the Nobel committee). Oslo: Aschehoug.

Lundestad, Geir (2015): *Fredens sekretær — Nobels fredpris gjennom 25 år.* Oslo: Kagge forlag.

Myrdal, Alva (1978): *The Game of Disarmament,* New York: Pantheon Books.

Norderval, Ingunn (2005): "The Nobel Peace Prize: How Have Women Fared?" *Scandinavian Review,* Autumn/Winter.

Norgren, Jill (1999): "Before It Was Merely Difficult: Belva Lockwood's Life in Law and Politics," *Journal of Supreme Court History,* Vol. 23, No. 1, pp. 16–42.

Norgren, Jill, (2002): "Lockwood in '84," *Wilson Quarterly,* Autumn, pp. 12–20.

Roosevelt, Eleanor (1933): *It's Up to the Women.* New York: Stokes.

Roosevelt, Eleanor (1937): *This Is My Story*. New York: Harper.

Roosevelt, Eleanor (1938): *This Troubled World*. New York: Kinsey.

Roosevelt, Eleanor (1940): *The Moral Basis of Democracy*. New York: Howell, Soskin.

Roosevelt, Eleanor (1949): *This I Remember*. New York: Harper & Brothers.

Rosika Schwimmer, World Patriot. (1947): Biografisk sketch, Rosika Schwimmer, in Schwimmer–Lloyd Collection Papers, New York Public Library.

Saue, Gerd Grønvold (1991): "Fredsfurien." En biografisk roman om Bertha von Suttner. Oslo: Aschehoug.

Saue, Gerd Grønvold (2001): JANE ADDAMS elsket og foraktet. Stavanger: Kvekerforlaget.

Schwimmer, Rosika (1941): *Union Now for Peace or War?* Chicago: The Campaign for World Government

Skard, Torild (2012): Maktens kvinner. Oslo: Universitetsforlaget.

Sørbye, Yngvild (2004): "Bedratt av historien?" Dagbladet, 10 October, p. 42.

Stenersen, Øivind, Ivar Libæk, and Asle Sveen (2001): *Nobels Fredspris: Hundre år for Fred. Prisvinnere 1901, 2000*. Oslo: Cappelen.

Stenersen, Øivind, Ivar Libæk, and Asle Sveen (2009): *The Nobel Peace Prize. One Hundred Years for Peace.*Addendum. Laureates 2001–2008. Oslo: Nobel Peace Center.

Stenersen, Øivind, Ivar Libæk, and Asle Sveen (2012): Nobels Fredspris. Vedlegg til Hundre År for Fred. Prisvinnere 2001–2011. Oslo: Nobels Fredssenter.

Veseth, Frøydis Eleonora (2000): "Women and the Nobel Peace Prize: Laureates and Nominees from 1901 to 1951." Oslo: Mastere's thesis, University of Oslo, spring 2000.

Williams, Jody (2013): *My Name Is Jody Williams*. Berkeley: University of California Press.

Wiltsher, Anne (1985): *Most Dangerous Women*. London: Pandora.

Winner, Julia Hull (1969): *Belva A. Lockwood*. Lockport, New York: Niagara County Historical Society.

Wittner, Lawrence S. (1987): "Taking Exception", *Wilson Quarterly*, Spring 1987.

Wynner, Edith (1965): "Out of the Trenches by Christmas," in *The Progressive*, December 1965.

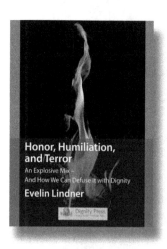
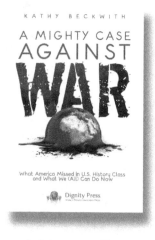

DECOLONIZING PEACE
220 pages; $16.00
ISBN 978-1-937570-15-6

DIGNITY
143 pages; $16.00
ISBN 978-1-937570-37-8

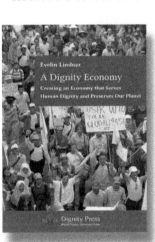

A DIGNITY ECONOMY
429 pages; $28.00
ISBN 978-1-937570-03-3

NO GREATER LOVE
132 pages; $9.00
ISBN 978-1-937570-65-1

CPSIA information can be obtained
at www.ICGtesting.com
Printed in the USA
FSHW020246310321
79964FS